MW00576753

Children's Mental Health Research

Children's Mental Health Research

The Power of Partnerships

Edited by

Kimberly Eaton Hoagwood

Peter S. Jensen

Mary McKay

Serene Olin

2010

OXFORD
UNIVERSITY PRESS

Oxford University Press, Inc., publishes works that further
Oxford University's objective of excellence
in research, scholarship, and education.

Oxford   New York
Auckland   Cape Town   Dar es Salaam   Hong Kong   Karachi
Kuala Lumpur   Madrid   Melbourne   Mexico City   Nairobi
New Delhi   Shanghai   Taipei   Toronto

With offices in
Argentina   Austria   Brazil   Chile   Czech Republic   France   Greece
Guatemala   Hungary   Italy   Japan   Poland   Portugal   Singapore
South Korea   Switzerland   Thailand   Turkey   Ukraine   Vietnam

Copyright © 2010 by Oxford University Press, Inc.

Published by Oxford University Press, Inc.
198 Madison Avenue, New York, New York 10016

www.oup.com

Oxford is a registered trademark of Oxford University Press

Library of Congress Cataloging-in-Publication Data

Children's mental health research: the power of partnerships / edited by Kimberly
Eaton Hoagwood . . . [et al.].
p.   cm.
Includes bibliographical references and index.
ISBN 978-0-19-530782-5
1. Child mental health—Research.   2. Child psychology—Methodology.
I. Hoagwood, Kimberly.
BF722.C45 2010
362.2072—dc22
2009027609

9 8 7 6 5 4 3 2 1

Printed in the United States of America
on acid-free paper

Contents

Case Studies of Collaboration Issues

Children's Mental Health Research

Chapter One

Redefining the Boundaries: Community–Research Partnerships to Improve Children's Mental Health

Kimberly Eaton Hoagwood, Peter S. Jensen, Mary McKay, and Serene Olin

M ichael Meaney (2001) describes the foolish perseveration with which the nature–nurture debate continues, despite decades of scientific work pointing to the interdependence and essential interplay between genes and the environment. He argues that the immense potential of the Human Genome Project to advance understanding of the biological processes that contribute to disease is coupled with an equally immense failure to develop conceptual models that cross the boundaries between genetic and environmental explanations about human behavior. Meaney (2001) points out that this now widely acknowledged artificial distinction and the ensuing debates continue because of assumptions made by proponents of each that confine understanding within narrow frameworks and dismiss alternative explanations for the same phenomenon.

Equally problematic distinctions and insularities have plagued the field of children's mental health services. Some of these debates pit arguments about the value of scientific findings against practice-based experiential learning; evidence-based practices against practice-based evidence; or system-of-care values against empirically validated interventions.

The fundamental premise of this book is that these distinctions inhibit the construction of an ethically valid, usable, and viable science. For example, the widely used phrase "evidence-based practices" has been framed as a set of practices that operate in contradistinction to system of care principles. Whereas evidence-based practices are understood as scientifically derived knowledge about specific interventions associated with specific improvements in children's behavioral or emotional functioning, the system of care is understood as a set of principles and values that guide delivery of child and family services. Said another way, evidence-based practices organize knowledge; the system of care organizes interpretation of knowledge based on fundamental and explicitly stated values. However, these are not competing paradigms. Rather, they are two separate but interdependent processes. The system-of-care framework enables scientific questions to be scaffolded with public health meaning and significance. It enables scientific thinking about what to study and why to be informed—and in some cases transformed—by ethical thinking. Likewise, system-of-care principles themselves can be transformed and reformed through scientific progress, as new ways of improving children's and families lives are uncovered. In other words, these are two interdependent ways of thinking about children's services and how to improve them.

The purpose of this book is to make explicit the implicit frameworks of researchers, community practitioners, parents or caregivers, and family advisors about models for creating sustained partnerships to improve knowledge about mental health services for children, adolescents, and their families. The authors of each chapter and the contributors to the casebook (see Chapter Five) provide specific examples of community–research partnerships that are contributing to the knowledge base about children's mental health. We emphasize the co-construction of the knowledge base through explicit models of partnership. We do so because the traditional research paradigms, based on unidirectional or linear models of knowledge construction, have been driven primarily by incremental and narrowly focused research questions. This traditional research framework has trivialized, if not ignored, the potential of community collaborations to enhance the validity and usefulness of scientific findings. Our hope is that by focusing a critical lens on these newer participatory paradigms, we can detect the contours of more meaningful dialectical exchanges among research and community partners.

PRINCIPLES OF COLLABORATION

Conceptually, the centerpiece for participatory action research (Argyris, Putnam, & Smith, 1985; Whyte, 1991) and empowerment research (Rappaport, 1981, 1994) has been collaboration among diverse community constituents. A widely accepted description of participatory action research is offered by Singer (1993):

> (1) [it] is developed through a "perpetual discussion" between experienced researchers and experienced community health educators and activists, and consequently (2) tends to reflect issues, concerns or pressing problems as perceived by members of the community being researched, that (3) is carried out by a heterogeneous research team; and (4) leads to recognition not only for the researchers but also for the community-based agency that sponsors it, as well as (5) a transfer of research skills to minority researchers, while (6) contributing to the intervention, public education, social development, advocacy and/or empowerment goals of the sponsoring agency. (p. 19)

The interpersonal dynamics set in motion by collaborative efforts are shaped in part by the model of collaboration, how the project is structured, the content around which the project revolves, the differing groups and communities involved, as well as less-malleable macro issues, such as social inequality, race relations, and local institutional history.

A number of challenges to creating research–community partnerships have been identified. These typically include issues such as lack of trust and respect; inequitable distribution of power and control; who represents the community; how the community is defined; and conflict around differing priorities, values, and roles (Altman, 1995; Israel, Schulz, Parker, & Becker, 1998; Linhorst, Hamilton, Young, & Eckert, 2002). Altman (1995) points out that explicit acknowledgment of areas of potential conflict may enhance their resolution. In recent years an increasing number of accounts of collaborative community research have accumulated and conceptual frameworks for explicating the collaboration concept have emerged (e.g., Altman, 1995; Israel et al., 1998; Wood & Gray, 1991). This literature clarifies how multifaceted the collaboration construct is. However, with rare exceptions, this literature has not been applied to constructing a stronger science base in children's mental health. One purpose of this volume is to redress this deficit.

The participatory research models described above are also consonant with the Theory of Communicative Action (1987) described by the philosopher-scientist Jurgen Habermas. The principles in this framework stipulate that justification for any community action should be based upon interpretation of normative standards through rational agreement among those who subscribe to those norms. Research–community partnerships, when guided by the principles of this theory, should therefore establish mini public spheres to ration power and share decision making, thus creating an ethical compact among the key stakeholders. Habermas' theory of communicative action and discourse ethics base the justification of norms by which actions shall be taken on uncoerced, rational agreement among those who will accept the norms. Through processes of reflective discussion, argumentation, and shared aspects of decision making, reasoned agreement can be reached.

Unfortunately, much of what passes for collaborations in children's mental health research has been either front-end or end-stage processes, where community groups are brought together at the beginning of a project, often through focus groups, to provide input for questions of terminology, or are involved after a project has been completed to disseminate findings. However, to create collaborations that will be sustainable, an ongoing and meaningful partnership must be established from beginning to end, such that shared decision making occurs throughout: that is, in the selection of aims, design, methods, measures development, implementation of the study, and dissemination of findings. This ethically grounded relationship can lead to sustained changes beyond the particular research project. It is under such circumstances that collaborations and their consequences—findings that are palatable, usable, ethical, and valid—can be most successful (Jensen, Hoagwood, & Trickett, 1999).

NOT YET TRANSLATABLE:
THE SCIENCE-TO-PRACTICE GAP

One reason why collaborative models are especially needed now is because knowledge about the etiology and course of children's mental health development and interventions to improve children's functioning exists but are rarely used. In fact, the gap between the extensive knowledge base and its applicability in real-world practice to improve the lives of children and families is widening. Studies by Weisz et al. have demonstrated that mental health interventions used to treat youth in everyday clinical practice are not only different from those studied in academic settings but also potentially less effective (Weisz, Donenberg, & Han, 1995; Weisz, Weiss, & Donenberg, 1992). Garland, Hurlburt, and Hawley (2006) have shown how effective components or strategies are used in usual care but with far less intensity than in evidence-based interventions. Weisz et al. (1992) found that the vast majority of studies supporting the effectiveness of psychotherapies were conducted in university, school, or laboratory settings, not routine health settings where the majority of children receive their care. The conditions of routine care are vastly different from the conditions under which most studies of effective interventions to improve children's mental health have been conducted.

Weisz and colleagues (Weisz et al., 1992; Weisz et al., 1995; Weisz & Jensen, 1999; Weisz, 2000, 2001) also identified some possible explanations for this disparity. One is that academic settings may be more conducive to documenting improvements simply because they have more resources. Providers may be better trained and have better equipment and supervision, making it a setting in which to deliver services. Another explanation is that treatments provided in academic settings may result in better outcomes because behavioral or cognitive-behavioral methods are more likely to be used there, and they constitute the largest proportion of the evidence base for psychosocial therapies for children. While studies are currently underway to examine how best to implement research-based interventions in routine settings and state systems (Asarnow et al., 2004; Hodges, 2004; North et al., 2008; Schoenwald, Kelleher, Weisz, & The Research Network on Youth Mental Health, 2008), the gaps between the exigencies of real-world health care and the demands of the evidence-based treatments deter easy uptake.

One problem that has contributed to this gap is that we rarely step back to examine the extent to which all necessary elements of scientific "proof" have been woven together to provide the necessary empirical fabric to demonstrate that the overarching theory has scientific support, that the theory-driven procedures have therapeutic effectiveness, and that postulated mechanisms for change have been identified (Jensen, 1999; Jensen, Weersing, Hoagwood, & Goldman, 2005; Kazdin, 2005; Weersing & Weisz, 2002). A number of competing explanations might equally be invoked to explain disparities. In many studies, for example, "nonspecific therapeutic factors," that is, the effects of attention, positive regard, and/or therapeutic alliance, may not be sufficiently examined or ruled out as alternative causal explanations (e.g., Jensen et al., 2005).

Taking a step back from current concepts of "efficacy," "effectiveness," and "evidence-based," as described now in numerous papers (Hinshaw & Silverman, 2008; Hoagwood, Burns, Kiser, Ringeisen, & Schoenwald, 2001; Weisz & Jensen, 1999), one may question whether further expansion of traditional linear and narrowly disciplinary research paradigms are sufficient to ensure that the knowledge base about effective practices for children is useful to families, acceptable to providers, and sustainable within communities.

FAMILY PARTNERSHIPS IN CHILDREN'S MENTAL HEALTH

Family/professional collaboration as a core feature of child mental health service delivery has been acknowledged since the 1980s within the Child and Adolescent Service System Program (CASSP) of the Center for Mental Health Services (Friesen, 1989, 1996; Stroul & Friedman, 1988). The federal government through SAMHSA has supported the development of an infrastructure within state mental health agencies to support consumer and family involvement in service planning, and most states have consumer or recipient offices to strengthen this involvement. Numerous family advocacy organizations now exist to support the needs of families with children who have emotional or behavioral problems more generally, and for those with specific psychiatric disorders (e.g., attention-deficit/hyperactivity disorder, bipolar disorders, depressive disorders, etc.) (Hoagwood et al., 2008). Simultaneously, there have been several major initiatives in primary care (through Institutes for Healthcare Improvement, for example) to reform health-care services nationally by positioning consumers, including families of children, centrally in health planning so that they are empowered to make decisions about their child's health care. These initiatives within both general health care and mental health care are leading to innovations in delivery, such as providing families with vouchers to function as case managers for their children's care. The movement away from office-based practice toward empowerment of consumers is likely to increase significantly over the next decade.

One reason that family involvement in service delivery has received more attention by state and local planners is that access to services is extremely difficult for most families and they face huge obstacles (e.g., long wait lists, multiple providers, conflicting diagnoses, and treatment plans). This is particularly the case in rural areas and among low-income, urban communities of color. The Surgeon General's *Mental Health Supplement Report on Race, Culture, and Ethnicity* (2001) underscored the importance of attending to issues of race, culture, and ethnicity if access to services is to be improved. Within low-income urban communities as many as 40% of youth exhibit significant mental health issues (Tolan & Henry, 1996). Yet even when minority youth and families initially access mental health services, high rates of "no shows" and attrition are notable: fewer than 40% of those initially requesting services actually are receiving them by the point of the expected third face-to-face contact (McKay, Stoewe, McCadam, & Gonzales, 1998). Improving meaningful involvement is essential to creating efficient and effective delivery systems.

Parental involvement has been shown to improve family retention, satisfaction, and to reduce caregiver strain (Dunst, Trivette, & Deal, 1988; Friesen, 1989; Hobbs, Walle, & Caldwell, 2004; Pinderhughes, 1982). Parental involvement may be intrinsically valuable as well, improving family's sense of altruism and giving back (Collins & Collins, 1990; DeChillo, 1993). However, parental collaboration in research as opposed to service delivery has proceeded more slowly. In part this may be a function of the traditional models for research that have largely emerged from academic and non–community-based environments, where input from "non-researchers" has been minimal. Yet this is changing. Some of the ways in which families have been involved in scientific activities in recent years include roles as advocates for research, as framers of research priorities, and as reviewers of research grant applications (Hoagwood, 2005). At a deeper level, many researchers are including family members as research associates based upon the hypotheses that the research is improved by engaging community leaders and family networks (Koroloff, Elliott, Koren, & Friesen, 1994). Finally, new roles for family members as consultants and advisors, providing feedback regarding instrumentation, study findings, and draft reports are being actively studied, using behavioral science models to understand parents as active agents of change (Olin et al., impress; Rodriguez et al., under review).

COMMUNITY-BASED SERVICES AND THE SYSTEM-OF-CARE FRAMEWORK

In the mid 1980s a series of initiatives focused on strengthening the community-based service system for children and adolescents. Under the auspices of the Child and Adolescent Service System Program (CASSP), a series of state grants were awarded by the National Institute of Mental Health (NIMH) to create youth and family bureaus within state systems. This was given principled footing through the creation of a model, called the system of care model, developed by Stroul and Friedman (1988). This model articulated a series of values, centered on maintaining children within their communities, coordinating services, involving families integrally in delivery and planning of treatments and services, and attending to the cultural relevance of services. The most important federal initiative to support community-based services has been the Comprehensive Community Mental Health Services for Children and Families (CMHSC).

Supported by the Center for Mental Health Services (CMHS) of the Substance Abuse and Mental Health Services Administration (SAMHSA), this program constitutes the single largest federal program supporting mental health services for youth with serious emotional or behavioral problems and is currently financed at more than $120 million per year.

The public-health emphasis on community-based services, family involvement, and the increasing reliance by consumers and providers on scientifically derived knowledge about effective practices has created a new set of challenges for the research community. These challenges include how to develop and strengthen contextually valid, ethically grounded, and widely acceptable research findings that can be readily translated into action within communities of practice. This book was written to support this goal.

ABOUT THIS BOOK

There are several reasons why we undertook this project. First, the concept of collaboration itself has so many different meanings that an initial task is to clarify some of the many ways in which it is currently used. Second, collaboration is a very context-bound concept; that is, whether it can work, how it works, and the issues in making it work are closely tied to the specific places, institutional arrangements, and cultural histories of the people and places involved. We provide examples to elucidate these contexts. Third, the very nature of the collaboration concept suggests a negotiation among parties about how work will unfold; it is a discussion about how to work together rather than the imposition of a formulaic structure on a negotiated process. Finally, the field of children's mental health has been subject to the diagnostic vicissitudes that have beset the psychiatric classification system in general (Jensen & Hoagwood, 2008). The tensions about the very meaning and definition of mental health in children underscore the importance of an increased collaboration with community members to improve understanding about children's mental health.

This is not a "how-to" book that provides formulas or specific recommendations for what to do in order to have a productive collaboration. Rather, the concepts, examples, and issues that are described can serve as a partner tool kit to spur new ways of thinking about collaboration. It is our hope that this book will increase awareness about the types of shared expertise that can yield productive and creative exchange of ideas and ultimately a more valid science. We hope, in short, that the concepts and principles of community collaboration, drawn from decades of critical work in fields outside of mental health, can be brought to bear on studies of children's mental health. By surfacing issues about the kinds of relationships that are possible within, between, and among members of a common culture, we hope to broaden the reach and deepen the relevancy of findings, and improve children's health outcomes.

This book was a true collaborative effort. In Chapter 2, Dr. Mary McKay and the CHAMP Collaborative Board describe the research challenges and opportunities in forging explicit partnerships with community partners throughout the many phases of research. Specific dimensions of collaboration in research with children and adolescents are highlighted. In Chapter 3, Dr. Nancy Koroloff and colleagues describe family perspectives on collaborative research and the ways in which collaboration can enhance the validity of the findings and the uptake of them. In Chapter 4, Dr. Robert Abramovitz and Mimi Abramovitz describe practitioner perspectives on collaborative research, the challenges to it, and specific examples of projects that have crafted creative solutions to those challenges. Chapter 5 is a casebook of specific examples drawn largely from interviews conducted with community researchers studying different aspects of children's health. The cases are intended to serve as a reference guide for those wanting to conduct collaborative community research. The conclusion in Chapter 6 by two of the editors to this volume reflects on how principles of collaboration can enliven, deepen, and validate scientific knowledge about children's mental health. In so doing, these principles also point to a future research agenda that links models of collaboration to the ethical endpoint of enhancing both the validity and usefulness of knowledge.

The authors and editors wish to thank the many families and advocates whose insights, perspectives, and energies on behalf of children's mental health have created so many opportunities for community partnerships. The Family Advocacy and Research Board (FAR Board) of New York City, chaired by Geraldine Burton, has contributed exceptionally valuable insights into partnership research for all of us.

References

Altman, D. G. (1995). Sustaining interventions in community systems: On the relationship between researchers and communities. *Health Psychology, 14,* 526–536.

Argyris, C., Putnam, R., & Smith, D. (1985). *Action science.* San Francisco: Jossey Bass.

Asarnow, J., Jaycox, L., Duan, N., Laborde, A. P., Rea, M. M., Tang, L., et al. (2004). Depression and role impairment among adolescents in primary care clinics. *Journal of Adolescent Health, 37,* 477–483.

Collins, B., & Collins, T. (1990). Parent professional relationships in the treatment of seriously emotionally disturbed children and adolescents. *Social Work, 35,* 522–527.

DeChillo, N. (1993). Collaboration between social workers and families of patients with mental illness. *Families in Society, 74,* 104–115.

Dunst, C. J., Trivette, C. M., & Deal, A. G. (1988). *Enabling and empowering families: Principles and guidelines for practice.* Cambridge, MA: Brookline Books.

Friesen, B. J. (1989). Parents as advocates for children and adolescents with serious emotional handicaps: Issues and directions. In R. M. Friedman, A. J. Duchnowski, & E. L. Henderson (Eds.) *Advocacy on behalf of children with serious emotional problems* (pp. 68–78). Springfield, IL: Charles C. Thomas.

Friesen, B. J. (1996). Family support in child and adult mental health. In G. H. S. Singer, L. E. Powers, & A. L. Olson (Eds.), *Redefining family support: Innovations in public–private partnerships* (Vol. 1, pp. 259–290). Family, community, and disability series. Baltimore, MD: Paul H. Brookes.

Garland, A. F., Hurlburt, M. S., & Hawley, K. M. (2006). Examining psychotherapy processes in a services research context. *Clinical Psychology: Science and Practice, 13*, 30–46.

Habermas, J. (1987). *The theory of communicative action* (Vol. 1 and 2). Boston: Beacon Press.

Hinshaw, S. P., & Silverman, W. K. (2008). The second special issue on evidence-based psychosocial treatments for children and adolescents: A 10-year update. *Journal of Clinical Child and Adolescent Psychology, 37*, 1–7.

Hoagwood, K., Burns, B. J., Kiser, L., Ringeisen, H., & Schoenwald, S. (2001). Evidence-based practices in child and adolescent mental health services. *Psychiatric Services, 52*, 1079–1089.

Hoagwood, K. E. (2005). Family-based services in children's mental health: A research review and synthesis. *Journal of Child Psychology and Psychiatry, 46*, 690–713.

Hoagwood, K. E., Green, E., Kelleher, K., Schoenwald, S., Rolls-Reutz, J., Landsverk, J., et al. (2008). Family advocacy, support and education in children's mental health: Results of a national survey. *Administration and Policy in Mental Health and Mental Health Services Research, 35*, 73–83.

Hobbs, S. A., Walle, D. L., & Caldwell, H. S. (2004). Maternal evaluation of social reinforcement and time-out: Effects of brief parent training. *Journal of Consulting and Clinical Psychology, 52*, 135–136.

Hodges, K. (2004). Using assessment in everyday practice for the benefit of families and practitioners. *Professional Psychology: Research and Practice, 35*, 449–456.

Israel, B. A., Schulz, A. J., Parker, E. A., & Becker, A. B. (1998). Review of community-based research: Assessing partnership approaches to improve public health. *Annual Review of Public Health, 19*, 173–202.

Jensen, P. (1999). Fact versus fancy concerning the multimodal treatment study for attention-deficit hyperactivity disorder. *Canadian Journal of Psychiatry, 44*, 975–980.

Jensen, P., & Hoagwood, K. (Eds). (2008). *Improving children's mental health through parent empowerment: A guide to assisting families.* New York: Oxford University Press.

Jensen, P. S., Hoagwood, K., & Trickett, E. (1999). Ivory tower or earthen trenches? Community collaborations to foster real-world research. *Journal of Applied Developmental Science, 3*, 206–212.

Jensen, P. S., Weersing, R., Hoagwood, K. E., & Goldman, E. (2005). What is the evidence for evidence-based treatments? A hard look at our soft underbelly. *Mental Health Services Research, 7*, 53–74.

Kazdin, A. E. (2005). Mechanisms of change in psychotherapy: Advances, breakthroughs, and cutting-edge research (do not yet exist). In R. R. Bootzin & P. M. McKnight (Eds.), *Strengthening research methodology: Psychological measurement and evaluation* (pp. 77–101). Washington, DC: American Psychological Association.

Koroloff, N. M., Elliott, D. J., Koren, P. E., & Friesen, B. J. (1994). Connecting low-income families to mental health services: The role of the family associate. *Journal of Emotional & Behavioral Disorders, 2*, 240–246.

Linhorst, D. M., Hamilton, G., Young, E., & Eckert, A. (2002). Opportunities and barriers to empowering people with severe mental illness through participation in treatment planning. *Social Work, 47*, 425–434.

McKay, M., Stoewe, J., McCadam, K., & Gonzales, J. (1998). Increasing access to child mental health services for urban children and their care givers. *Health and Social Work, 23*, 9–15.

Meaney, M. J. (2001). Nature, nurture, and the disunity of knowledge. *Annals of the New York Academy of Sciences, 935*, 50–61.

North, M. S., Gleacher, A. A., Radigan, M., Greene, L., Levitt, J. M., Chassman, J., & Hoagwood, K. (2008). Evidence-Based Treatment Dissemination Center (EBTDC): Bridging the research-practice gap in New York State. *Report on Emotional and Behavioral Disorders in Youth, 8*(1), 499–504.

Olin, S., Hoagwood, K. E., Rodriguez, J., Ramos, B., Burton, G., Pen, M., Crowe, M., Radigan, M., & Jensen, P. The application of behavior change theory to family-based services: Improving parent empowerment in children's mental health. *Journal of Child and Family Studies.*

Pinderhughes, C.A. (1982). Paired therapeutic bonding. *Current Psychiatric Therapies, 21*, 51–58.

Rappaport, J. (1981). In praise of paradox: A social policy of empowerment over prevention. *American Journal of Community Psychology, 9*, 1–25.

Rappaport, J. (1994). Empowerment as a guide to doing research: Diversity as a positive value. In E. J. Trickett, R. J. Watts, & D. Birman (Eds.), *Human diversity: Perspectives on people in context* (pp. 359–382). San Francisco: Jossey-Bass.

Rodriguez, J., Burton, G., Crowe, M., Ramos, B., Olin, S., Mehta, S., Radigan, M., & Hoagwood, K. Parent-to-parent support and engagement in children's mental health: The development and implementation of a parent empowerment program. Manuscript under review.

Schoenwald, S. K., Kelleher, K., Weisz, J. R., & The Research Network on Youth Mental Health. (2008). Building bridges to evidence-based practice: The MacArthur Foundation Child System and Treatment Enhancement Projects (Child STEPs). *Administration and Policy in Mental Health and Mental Health Services Research, 35*, 66–72.

Singer, M. (1993). Knowledge for use: Anthropology and community-centered substance abuse. *Social Science Medicine, 37*, 15–25.

Stroul, B. A., & Friedman, R. M. (1988). Principles for a system of care: Putting principles into practice. *Children Today, 17*, 11–15.

U.S. Public Health Service (2001). The Surgeon General's Mental Health Supplement on Culture, Race and Ethnicity. Department of Health and Human Services. Washington DC.

Tolan, P. H., & Henry, D. (1996). Patterns of psychopathology among urban poor children: Comorbidity and aggression effects. *Journal of Consulting and Clinical Psychology, 64*, 1094–1099.

Weersing, R. V., & Weisz, J. R. (2002). Community clinic treatment of depressed youth: Benchmarking usual care against CBT clinical trials. *Journal of Consulting and Clinical Psychology, 70*, 299–310.

Weisz, J. R. (2000). Agenda for child and adolescent psychotherapy research: On the need to put science into practice. *Archives of General Psychiatry, 57*, 837–838.

Weisz, J. R. (2000). Lab-clinic differences and what we can do about them: Linking research and practice to enhance our public impact. *Newsletter of the Division of Clinical Child Psychology.*

Weisz, J. R., Donenberg, G. R., & Han, S. S. (1995). Child and adolescent psychotherapy outcomes in experiments versus clinics: Why the disparity? *Journal of Abnormal Child Psychology, 23,* 83–106.

Weisz, J. R., & Jensen, P. S. (1999). Efficacy and effectiveness of psychotherapy and pharmacotherapy with children and adolescents. *Mental Health Services Research, 1,* 125–158.

Weisz, J. R., Weiss, B., & Donenberg, G. R. (1992). The lab versus the clinic: Effects of child and adolescent psychotherapy. *American Psychologist, 47,* 1578–1585.

Whyte, G. (1991). Diffusion of responsibility: Effects on the escalation tendency. *Journal of Applied Psychology, 76,* 408–415.

Wood, D. J., & Gray, B. (1991). Toward a comprehensive theory of collaboration. *Journal of Applied Behavioural Science, 27,* 139–162.

Chapter Two

Collaborating with Consumers, Providers, Systems, and Communities to Enhance Child Mental Health Services Research

Mary McKay, Peter S. Jensen, and The CHAMP Collaborative Board*

Child mental health service delivery systems need to maximize family participation.

— CHAMP Collaborative Board

Interagency collaboration is necessary for efficient child mental health service delivery.

— CHAMP Collaborative Board

Child mental health services researchers must partner with "real world" providers in order to ensure transportability of services to community-based settings.

— CHAMP Collaborative Board

Key stakeholders must be involved in order to develop culturally and contextually sensitive child mental health services.

— CHAMP Collaborative Board

Over the last two decades, child mental health services researchers have been encouraged to collaborate with youth who are mental health consumers, family members, providers, system administrators, mental health funders, and local communities in order to enhance the delivery of accessible, culturally and contextually relevant, effective child mental health services. Consumer advocacy organizations, funding bodies, and political figures are encouraging child mental health researchers to maximize family participation in research studies, effect and

---

* CHAMP (Collaborative HIV Prevention and Adolescent Mental Health Project) Collaborative Board is a consortium of parents, youth, school staff members, and university-based researchers in Bronx, New York.

study interagency coordination, partner with service providers in community-based settings, and involve key stakeholders in the research process (Federation of Families, 1998, 1999; National Alliance for the Mentally Ill, 1994, 1999). Calls to increase collaboration among key stakeholders are grounded in the serious need to support the mental health of youth nationally (Elliott, Koroloff, Koren, & Friesen, 1998; Jensen, Hoagwood, & Trickett, 1999; Jivanjee & Friesen, 1997; Knitzer, 1989, 1996, 2000) and to create an ethical science by which to guide service delivery and future research efforts.

Support for collaborative research efforts has emerged in response to the recognition that children and adolescents continue to experience mental health difficulties at alarming rates (McCabe et al., 1999; Murray & Lopez, 1996; Tolan & Henry, 1996; U.S. Department of Health and Human Services, 2000). In the early 1980s, Knitzer (1982) indicted the child mental health service delivery system as failing to respond to youth in serious need of mental health care. Two decades later, rates of child mental health difficulties remain at alarming levels with an estimated 17% to 26% of youth in need of mental health care across the United States (Brandenburg et al., 1987; McCabe et al., 1999; Tuma, 1989). Within low-income, urban communities of color, rates of child mental health need have been found to be even higher with as many as 40% of youth exhibiting significant mental health issues (Tolan & Henry, 1996). Yet, despite the presence and recognition of significant need among our nation's children, evidence continues to accumulate that children are not receiving adequate mental health care (Burns et al., 1995; Kadzin, 1993; McKay, McCadam, & Gonzales, 1996; McKay, Stoewe, McCadam, & Gonzales, 1998).

Even when youth do have contact with the current child mental health service system, they are still likely to receive care that is not matched to their need or that lacks a substantial evidence base (Kadzin, 1993; Jensen et al., 1999; Weisz, 2000). There is a clear need to increase the number of effective child mental health services overall, as its evidence base lags behind the adult mental health field substantially (Arnold et al., 1997; Hibbs & Jensen, 1996; Institute of Medicine, 1989; U. S. Department of Health and Human Services, 2000; Vitiello & Jensen, 1997). Further, only in the last decade has the child mental health services research field focused on the development of services that can be delivered in "real-world" settings by community-based providers rather than in tightly controlled research settings (Henggeler, Cunningham, Pickrel, & Schoenwald, 1996; Weisz et al., 1995; Weisz, Hawley, Pilkonis, Woody, & Follette, 2000). Attention to issues of transportability of services to youth, families, and communities experiencing need is critical if rates of child mental health difficulties are to be reduced. In sum, calls for increased collaboration among those that are invested in the mental health of youth are based upon difficult realities, including the fact that the mental health of youth has not substantially improved nationally, nor have effective services been developed at the rate necessary to impact those in need, particularly those youth experiencing the most severe problems.

Although calls for increasing the number of collaborative research efforts have been made, there is still relatively little guidance available to researchers interested in increasing the level of collaboration within their research studies. Therefore, this chapter will outline key principles of collaboration that can guide efforts to involve consumers, family members, providers, administrators, and community members more fully in child mental health services research efforts. Next, opportunities for collaboration across the research process, from the development of guiding research questions, to study methods and procedures, to interpretation of study results and dissemination activities will be highlighted. Examples of the challenges that arise in collaborative efforts with youth and their families, providers, systems, and communities are also discussed. Finally, a discussion of next steps for child mental health services research is offered.

FOUNDATION PRINCIPLES OF COLLABORATION

As was discussed in the previous chapter, collaborative research efforts are not new and have their basis in social science research traditions that span decades. Although collaborative efforts have been characterized in numerous ways, there are at least five core principles that could serve to guide strong collaborations between university-based researchers and child mental health constituents. Figure 2.1 provides a summary of five core principles that can impact both the process and outcome of collaborative efforts. More specifically, collaborative efforts can be characterized by the extent to which there are *(1)* agreement and

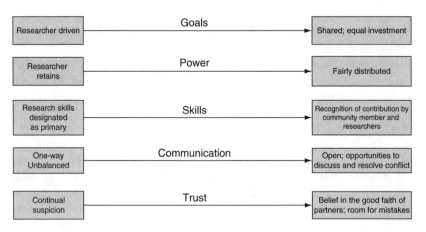

Figure 2.1 Principles of collaborative child mental health services research efforts.

investment in shared goals; *(2)* equitable distribution of power, including fair involvement in decision making and opportunities to change aspects of the research process; *(3)* recognition of skills and expertise associated with both university training and community experience; *(4)* ongoing opportunities for communication based upon commitment to honest exchanges and willingness to raise concerns without blame; and *(5)* trust.

As indicated in Figure 2.1, each of these collaborative principles can be assessed along a continuum, with the far right-hand side being defined as the most intensive level of collaboration, while, the left-hand side mirrors low levels of collaboration between researchers and key child mental health stakeholders. This continuum is meant to serve as a guide to child mental health researchers as they evaluate their current collaborative efforts and consider the potential benefits of increasing the level of collaboration in future studies.

Shared Goals

First, the development of shared goals that are acceptable to both researchers and key stakeholders is necessary to ensure productive collaborative efforts (Israel, Schulz, Parker, & Becker, 1998; Labonte, 1994; Reed & Collins, 1994). Clearly, a common goal shared by child mental health services researchers and consumers, families, providers, and communities is the need to support the mental health of children. However, specifying the goals that will guide specific partnerships and focus research efforts can require a melding of perspectives and priorities that often appear divergent initially. For example, while both researchers and constituents would agree that children are not gaining access to needed services, solutions to this situation might differ within the partnership. The primary task of the university-based researcher is to generate new knowledge. Therefore, from the perspective of the researcher, studies that specify the obstacles that block service access or those that rigorously test interventions to increase access to care might be seen as important goals in order to understand how the service delivery systems needs to be changed to support youth in need.

Partners representing families, on the other hand, might approach the goal of increasing access to services for children from a different perspective. For example, families might legitimately believe that we already know much about obstacles to care and that widespread change to service system entry procedures are needed immediately. In fact, much of the support for the system of care movement came from family advocacy groups highlighting the fact that children were not receiving appropriate services due to gaps in coordination and the lack of a single point of entry for care (Friedman, 1996). Members of collaborative partnerships must wrestle with these divergent perspectives in order to negotiate goals that incorporate an appreciation for the sense of urgency that families often feel relative to needed changes in child mental health service systems, while also respecting the need to test the impact of changes carefully to ensure that they have the intended outcomes for youth.

Distribution of Power

Not only do shared goals and the processes by which these goals are achieved have to be decided upon, but decisions regarding how power is distributed in relation to the decision-making process is a critical concern in the formation of collaborative partnerships. Wood and Gray (1991) identify sharing of power as being critical to the creation of longstanding partnerships. Many authors have voiced concern that unless power is shared among partners, rather than being largely held by university-based researchers, then the collaboration is essentially a facade (Callahan, Rademacher, Hildreth, & Hildreth, 1998; Hatch, Moss, Saran, & Presley-Cantrell, 1993; Israel et al., 1998; Roe, Minkler, & Saunders, 1995). Researchers and mental health stakeholders can exercise their power in unique ways within collaborative research endeavors. For example, the power of researchers is often in the form of very specialized expertise (e.g., research and proposal writing skills) and access to research funding. Providers or communities, on the other hand, exercise their power by both supporting research efforts and opening access to participants or by blocking opportunities to conduct research within their settings or communities. Ideally, collaborative partnerships bring their collective power to bear in order to achieve the agreed upon goals.

However, as the level of collaboration intensifies, there is also recognition that each party has some level of veto power and that compromise will often be necessary to proceed forward. For example, child mental health providers may insist on having opportunities for input regarding how research procedures will be implemented in their agency. Researchers might need to adjust to providers' "reality" as to what procedures are possible within the setting. In negotiations related to power, it is important for each partner to articulate at the beginning of the collaboration where compromise is possible from their perspective and also identify areas that are nonnegotiable.

Recognition of Skills and Competencies

Distributing power among partners requires mutual respect for the skills and competencies of each collaborative partner. An important activity early in the partnership might be to concretely identify what skills and competencies each partner brings to the collaboration (Madison et al., in press). For example, in collaborations with community members, there could be recognition that community members have knowledge regarding acceptable recruitment strategies or cultural practices that could be incorporated into innovative service delivery approaches. Child mental health service providers, on the other hand, might be able to articulate the complex needs of their client populations and common barriers to the use of evidence-based approaches. These skills are critical in collaborative research efforts and are more important than in traditional research approaches, where accommodation of science to community context does not occur.

Communication

The development of shared goals, processes by which power is shared, and respect for individual and collective skills all require ongoing communication between members of the partnership and a willingness to engage in productive conflict resolution. This takes time. For example, a "researcher needs skills and competencies in addition to those required in research design and methods, for example, listening, communication (e.g., use of language that is understandable and respectful), group process, team development, negotiation, conflict resolution, understanding and competency to operate in multicultural contexts, ability to be self-reflective and admit mistakes, capacity to operate within different power structures, and humility" (Israel et al., 1998, p. 187). Although some researchers clearly have the collaborative skills that foster open dialogue, many other researchers have called upon a neutral party or collaborative convener to facilitate ongoing communication (Franco et al., 2006; Madison et al., in press; McKay et al., 2000). Whether the researchers attempt to facilitate the collaborative process by themselves or rely on an outside facilitator, the dialogue between partners needs time to evolve and can be expected to consume hours of partners' time.

Trust

Closely linked with the necessity for ongoing opportunities to communicate is one of the key elements of collaborative partnership: that of the building of trust between members (Friend & Cook, 1990; Singer, 1993; Wood & Gray, 1991). How does trust or a lack of trust manifest itself within child mental health focused partnerships? Concretely, comments such as "You just don't understand" or "Why do you want to work with our community, families, agency?" are often heard. Unfortunately, many families, providers, and communities can recount prior negative experiences with university-based research projects (Galbraith et al., 1996; Madison et al., in press; Stevenson & White, 1994). There is often substantial concern regarding researchers' motivation to conduct children's research projects and questions regarding whether the researchers are committed to the setting or community once research funding is expended. Therefore, researchers need to be prepared to achieve credibility with constituents and often must engage in tasks, such as volunteer grant writing or attending community events to demonstrate their commitment to the partnership.

The incorporation of these core collaborative principles into child mental health services research projects requires extensive commitments of time, energy, and resources on the part of both university-based researchers and key constituents, including potentially consumers, family members, providers, systems, and community representatives (Rogers & Palmer-Erbs, 1994). Further, as a researcher moves to the right on the continuum, there must also be an incremental shift in the willingness to give up some degree of power and control.

Finally, though these five principles are meant to guide collaborative research efforts, they may not be sufficiently specific to guide the development of collaborative partnerships and to maintain these coalitions over the long term. Therefore, partnerships have often articulated behavioral guidelines for both research and community partners that are intended to maintain collaborative processes, particularly during times of conflict. Table 2.1 outlines an example of such principles that guide a partnership testing a service integration model (Hooper-Briar & Lawson, 1994).

Table 2.1 Guidelines for Development and Maintenance of Collaborative Efforts

- Finger pointing and blaming are not allowed.
- Everyone is both part of the problem and part of the solution. All participants must be seen as doing the best that they can do, including children, parents, and professionals.
- Specialized language, abbreviations, and acronyms are not allowed in the dialogue.
- It is everyone's responsibility to reframe and rethink the ways in which today's problems and needs present opportunities. How we can turn a potential crisis into a preventive action strategy is everyone's question and responsibility.
- There is more than enough work for everyone, so let's not make "turf" an issue. Rather than turf battles, we pledge to seek shared ways to divide up the work and even modify our conventional roles.
- Even then, there probably will not be enough hands on deck. We pledge to recruit more stakeholders, including children and families, into the change process.
- Power will be shared, not monopolized. It must be used in win–win rather than win–lose ways.
- When a crisis occurs, we will not blame either victims or professionals; we pledge to look first for flaws in our policies and services.
- We deputize the following person (s) to speak for the group; we pledge to avoid jealousy for the publicity and attention generated.
- We pledge to be kind to each other and to the children and families we serve. We know that collaboration is impossible without an ethic of kindness, caring, and concern.
- We pledge to build from these agreements among individuals, formal agreements among our agencies and organizations, especially our schools, health and human service agencies, and other governmental organizations.
- We promise to remember that, insofar as poverty, homelessness, and unemployment are root causes of the needs and problems of our most vulnerable children and families, we need to plan simultaneously for community and job development.
- We promise to keep the needs, problems, interests, and aspirations of children, youth, and families at the center of our work, remembering that they are the reason for our individual and collective efforts.

Source: Hooper-Briar and Lawson, 1994.

In addition to having the ability to work with key stakeholders on developing working guidelines, child mental health services researchers are called upon to develop a number of other collaborative research skills, including helping collaborators develop research competencies. Examples of such skills are highlighted in Figure 2.2.

More specifically, in order to increase the level of collaboration between university-based researchers and child mental health constituents, shifts in both researchers' and community members' attitudes and behavior are necessary. For example, community stakeholders must have at least some willingness to overcome negative attitudes about research, as well as an openness to learning more about research activities (Galbraith et al., 1996; Madison et al., in press). In order to accomplish this, opportunities for community members to learn about the advantages and limitations of specific research designs and methods are needed. Concepts such as random assignment and standardization must become familiar, along with the advantages and limitations of validated instruments (McKay, McCadam, & Gonzales, 1997). Recently, a literature has emerged that provides some guidance regarding how to prepare community-based partners to develop research-supportive skills. Several efforts have focused on the development of workshop series or training opportunities that concentrate on the development of leadership and interpersonal skills, as well as research familiarity (Franco et al., 2006; Madison et al., in press; McKay, Paikoff et al., 1997).

Further, collaboration requires child mental health services constituents to take risks and share information honestly with researchers regarding community needs, perceptions of research, ideas regarding cultural values, and contextual norms. Such information exchange can be considered a significant risk given the serious

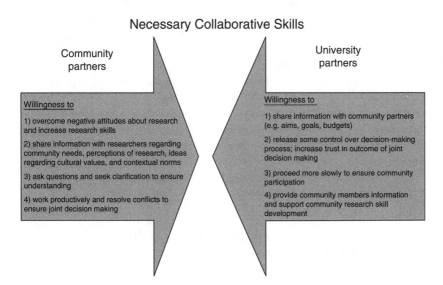

Figure 2.2 Accommodations necessary for university and community partners.

concern that vulnerable communities often have that researchers will use this information to reinforce negative stereotypes about the community and its members (Krauss, 1998; McKay et al., 2000; Stevenson & White, 1994). Finally, community partners must be willing to ask questions and seek clarification to ensure understanding. This is necessary in order to work productively and resolve conflicts to ensure joint decision making.

In addition to community partners, university-based researchers need to enhance collaborative skills. Collaborative partnerships begin with a willingness on the part of the researcher to share information and expertise generously. Necessary information includes sharing knowledge regarding a research study's specific aims, primary hypotheses, advantages and limitations of research procedures, and budgets. In order to build a critical level of communication and trust, researchers must proceed slowly to ensure community participation and understanding. This often requires the researcher to build in a longer period of start-up to ensure that community participation has been accomplished prior to the beginning of research activities. In collaborative research efforts, researchers are often called upon to accept the substantial responsibility to provide ongoing training and support as constituents advance in their research and collaborative skill development (Gasch et al., 1991; Madison, McKay, Paikoff, & Bell, 2000; Madison et al., in press).

Thus far, we have discussed attitudes and behaviors on the part of both university-based research and collaborators that form the basis of a working, collaborative relationship. This relationship has also been characterized as an "ethical compact" whereby investigators and community participants work jointly to understand and/or intervene with the mental health difficulties of children within a specific community. See final chapter for further discussion. This ethically grounded relationship will frequently transcend the time and space boundaries of the more narrowly defined, specific research project, and it is under such circumstances that collaborations are most successful (Jensen, 2000; Schorr, 1989). This view of research partnerships directly counters what community participants have, at times, referred to as "research hit-and-run," those experiences with investigators that are short lived, where the community benefits little, and there is no investigator/community contact beyond the duration of a particular research project. Researchers with a short-term goal to test the efficacy of a given program, and who depart once their research resources have ended, are likely to leave in their wake communities and citizens with initially heightened expectations and rekindled hopes, followed by bitter disappointment and hardened commitments to refuse future research involvements.

OPPORTUNITIES FOR COLLABORATION ACROSS THE RESEARCH PROCESS

Opportunities to collaborate with child mental health constituents occur across the research process as is modeled in Figure 2.3.

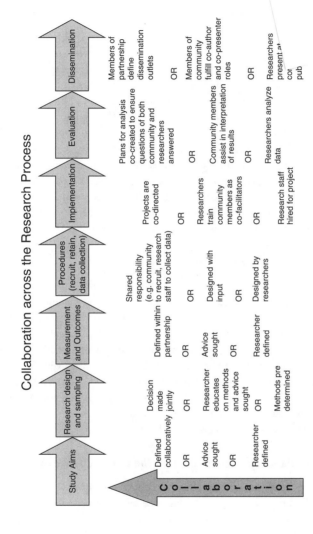

Figure 2.3 Opportunities for collaboration across the research process.

tch and colleagues (1993) proposed a model to characterize the depth
intensity of collaborative efforts across the research process. As is noted in
Figure 2.3, it is possible to increase the depth of collaboration at any or all points
in the research process.

Low-Intensity Collaborations

Hatch proposes that initial collaborative efforts often begin with a relatively less
intense form of collaboration whereby researchers consult with persons, either for
advice or consent, representing agencies or institutions within a specific community. At the next stage of increasingly collaborative efforts, researchers identify key
informants from the community (e.g. representatives from churches, business,
etc.) and seek acceptance of the research project. Although this group of key
informants is considered to be more representative of community stakeholders,
the research agenda and, therefore, the decision-making power, remains with the
researcher. As collaboration proceeds, influential community leaders might be
sought out by investigators to provide advice and guidance at a particular point in
a research study. Often they are asked to sit on ongoing advisory boards. Further,
their assistance is actively sought so that community members can be hired by the
project as paid staff and fulfill positions, such as interviewers or recruiters.

Moderate- to High-Intensity Collaborations

Hatch and colleagues (1993) indicate that although additional input is sought as
collaborative efforts intensify, key decisions regarding who has ultimate control
over research questions and decisions regarding research methods, procedures, and
interpretation of study results are critical. At the highest level of collaboration, the
research partners, both university and community based, work together to develop
the focus of the research and an action agenda. Then both university and community partners are responsible for pursuing these shared goals. At the most
intense level of collaboration, there is true partnership between community and
university in shared decision making and recognition of the specific talents of both
university and community members.

Examples of Collaborative Efforts across the Research Process

As was discussed earlier, collaborative research efforts are not new, but rather have
been in place in various forms for decades. The same is true for the child mental
health services research field in that many researchers are actively engaged in
collaborative partnerships, which are changing the nature of research across
the entire process. For example, researchers are actively collaborating with
families and service providers regarding innovative service delivery strategies
for youth with serious emotional disturbance (Armstrong & Evans, 1992; Evans,
Armstrong, Thompson, & Lee, 1994; Koroloff, Elliott, Koren, & Friesen, 1994;

Ruffolo, 1998), youth exhibiting disruptive behavioral difficulties (Henggeler, 1999; McKay, Gonzales, Quintana, Kim, & Abdul-Adil, 1999; Santos et al., 1995), and youth needing care within a range of settings, including outpatient clinics (Brent, Bridge, Johnson, & Connolly, 1998; Brent et al., 1998; Weisz, 2000; Weisz & Hawley, 1998), school-based settings (Atkins et al., 1998; Catron, Harris, & Weiss, 1998), and primary care health settings (Kelleher, 1999).

More specifically, multiple researchers are involved in collaborative efforts to increase *recruitment and retention* in child mental health services research projects by incorporating consumers as paid staff or community members as interviewers or recruiters. These community representatives, sometimes also referred to as paraprofessionals, fulfill liaison roles between youth and families in need and the mental health service system (Elliott et al., 1998; Koroloff et al., 1994; McCormick et al., 2000). In some cases, consumers are the first contact that a family has with a specific experimental mental health service, preventive intervention, or longitudinal research project. The involvement of collaborators in these roles has been associated with significant increases in involvement by potential participants (Elliott et al., 1998; Koroloff et al., 1994; McCormick et al., 2000).

In other cases, efforts are underway to facilitate the *implementation* of innovative service delivery approaches. For example, child mental health services might be co-delivered by providers and other professionals, such as teachers (Atkins et al., 1998) or parents (McKay et al., 2000). More specifically, a model for school-based mental health services that relies upon the development of strong collaborative relationships between mental health service providers and urban elementary school teachers is currently being tested (Atkins et al., 1998). This model, referred to as PALS (Positive Attitudes toward Learning in Schools), attempts to reduce the early behavioral difficulties of youth by working directly with teachers to establish interventions that are tailored to the needs of individual teachers and classrooms. The PALS service delivery model integrates interventions into ongoing school routines and builds upon existing resources (Atkins et al., 1998).

Also at the macro level, researchers are actively engaged in partnerships with community representatives, local and state governments, and service delivery organizations in dissemination of evidence-based child mental health services (Catalano, Arthur, Hawkins, Berglund, & Olson, 1998; Henggeler, 1999; Kellam et al., 2000). For example, one of the child mental health service delivery approaches consistently associated with positive outcomes for youth exhibiting serious conduct related difficulties and self-injurious behaviors is multi-systemic therapy (MST) (Henggeler, 1999; Henggeler, Schoenwald, & Pickrel, 1995; Santos et al., 1993). The delivery of MST to youth and families in need is guided by the nine principles that are meant to ensure adherence to the intervention protocol while simultaneously assisting in the transportability of this service delivery mechanism to new settings nationally and internationally. The MST principles serve to guide and standardize training of service providers in the implementation of MST within large-scale tests of the model. Within these broader trials, collaboration has been necessary at not only the family level but also at the level of real-world providers and mental health service delivery organizations and funders of mental health programs.

Collaboration within research studies can increase the relevance of research findings and maximize the likelihood those findings will be generalizable, thus enhancing external validity. Traditional academic research projects in general focus on enhancing internal validity, with the implicit assumption that once results have been generated, the external validity can be enhanced by gradual extension of the studies to increasingly diverse populations and settings. So a typical process in traditional academic studies would be to apply the design and methods from a rigorous university-based study and move it into a more diverse setting to examine the impact of the intervention when applied to more heterogeneous population in the "real world". However "real world" research begins with a different premise: that any intervention to be ultimately usable *within* communities has to be feasible and palatable to those communities. We suggest that the implicit paradigm that has guided much of children's mental health research, including privileging internal validity at the expense of external validity, is conceptually limiting. It has set an upper boundary on the empirical benefits that might be demonstrated from research programs. Consequently, effective community-research partnerships balance the demands of both internal and external validity.

To do so requires beginning with a different end point. Investigators wishing to undertake studies in communities begin with the goal of developing services that will be sensible (e.g., face valid), feasible, flexible, and palatable. Primacy is given to these four parameters. Once these are in place, additional methods to ensure internal validity are important and needed.

For example, developing a typical program of research with a university setting on an intervention generally begins with identifying conceptual or theoretical issues that are unresolved (involving mechanisms of change, for example), and that may better explain the findings. While this approach is clearly important for sharpening basic understanding about human behavior, it is not designed to enhance the fit of the intervention within an applied setting. To do so requires paying attention to a different set of issues—those that are relevant to the community in which the intervention is targeted. Ignoring the feedback of community. Early in the course of developing interventions with community partners, feedback from the partners is essential to the ultimate acceptability and success of the research (Hoagwood, Burns, Kiser, Ringeisen & Schoenwald, 2001). While this is a time-consuming process, requiring many hours of researcher's time with community partners, if this step is ignored, the ultimate fit of the intervention to the community and the ultimate acceptance of the finding will be threatened.

Ensuring That Study Methods Have the Necessary Flexibility to Fit Local Needs/Circumstances

Medicine does not use a one-size-fits-all approach in treating illness. Medication dosages are tailored to body size, and even surgical procedures are modified to fit the need of the patient. Interventions developed within effective community research collaborations, while adhering to core and key *principles* that make the intervention effective, also must allow the intervention to fit the specific needs, local resources, and customs of that community. Thus, while the principles and specific aspects of the intervention may remain relatively constant across communities, specific strategies to make the intervention fit within the resources and needs of the community may vary. Such considerations may lead to modifications in pace, ordering, timing, and delivery vehicles of interventions. The presence of these factors allowing local adaptations, coupled with core elements/principles of change, might together constitute the necessary *and* sufficient ingredients to deliver a reasonably effective intervention across multiple settings, outside of university-based settings, and with a variety of community partners.

Modifications of Research Methods

The degree to which a truly collaborative investigator/community partnership evolves may lead to necessary modifications or different research methods. As noted earlier, in real-world settings, the generally accepted, well-controlled, tightly constrained aspects of traditional research designs are often not feasible. For example, random assignment to a placebo condition may not be acceptable and a wait-list control condition may be used instead. Moreover, given the importance of understanding the impact of ecological factors in real-world settings, and the complexity of these multiple interacting but "uncontrolled" variables, analytic approaches and research designs for these settings must explore new methods, in order to fully capture the developmental phenomena under study. These methods must take into account that it frequently is not just some characteristic of a child that should be the object of study, but the contextually and historically shaped *transactions* that take place between the child and his/her larger environment of family, peers, schools, and neighborhoods. Under some circumstances more ethnographic or qualitative methods may be necessary to enable the voices and perspectives of citizens to be fully heard in the research. Also, if the research addresses topics such as racially sensitive information, special considerations (e.g., interviewer race) may need to be entertained that move beyond the interpersonal dynamics between researcher and citizen, accommodating issues such as group identities into research methods and design.

Such issues are not new. Research methods shape the endpoints of knowledge. Insofar as they are superficial or constraining, important dynamic processes may well be neglected. Horkheimer and Adorno (1972) wrote that "the refusal of science to handle in an appropriate way the problems connected with the social process has led to superficiality in method and content, and this superficiality, in turn, has found expression in the neglect of dynamic relations between various areas with which science deals, while also affecting in quite varied ways the practice of the disciplines."

COLLABORATIVE RESEARCH IN "ACTION"

Consumer Collaboration

Few examples of collaboration with youth exist within the child mental health literature. However, important lessons have been learned from research efforts involving adults with mental illness as research partners. For example, adults with mental illness, or consumer advocates, as play key roles in the development, implementation, and evaluation of Assertive Community Treatment program (Dixon, 2000; Lehman et al., 1999). For example, consumer advocates are described as having "street smarts," meaning that they have personal information that allows them to reach out effectively to client populations and also effectively advocate for clients within larger systems, including mental health. Further, consumer advocates are described as enhancing the research project by bringing excellent engagement skills that allow for maximum client participation. Consumer advocates are also viewed as critical in creating opportunities for peer support, providing positive role modeling, addressing issues of stigma, and educating co-workers, including mental health professionals (Dixon, 2000).

The involvement of consumer advocates also presents a unique set of challenges to the researchers. First, the role of a consumer advocate is not well defined in the literature; therefore, a clear mandate for the consumer advocate needs to be negotiated, and the feasibility and potential therapeutic benefit of the role needs to be considered and negotiated. Also, issues need to be resolved relating to how consumer advocates should be supervised and by whom. The presence of the consumer advocate also presents research challenges, such as location of methods to identify to what extent the consumer advocates were fulfilling their roles and the related impact of their contact with study participants (Dixon, 2000).

Beyond the experiences of ACT, numerous efforts involve consumers in program planning around vocational issues for women with serious mental illness (Pickett-Schenk, Cook, & Laris, 2000; Pickett, Heller, & Cook, 1998), in the area of youth violence with gang members (Spergel & Grossman, 1997), and in efforts to reduce HIV and mental health risk (Franco et al., 2006; McKay et al., 2000).

Collaboration with Family Members

Within the field of child mental health services research there is a strong tradition of collaborating closely with family members. Much of the urgency for collaborative research approaches has been created by strong family advocacy organizations, such as the Federation of Families, National Alliance for the Mentally Ill (NAMI), and Children and Adults with Attention-Deficit/Hyperactivity Disorder (CHADD).

There is growing recognition that family/professional collaboration is an important feature of child mental health service delivery (Collins & Collins, 1990; DeChillo, 1993). However, full family collaboration in research activities has proceeded more slowly, as described more fully in the next chapter. There is a range of ways that collaboration with families can occur within child mental health research studies. These include involving families in setting research priorities and reviewing research grant applications. At a deeper level, many researchers are including family members as research associates based upon the hypotheses that the research is improved by engaging community leaders and family networks. Finally, new roles for family members as consultants and advisors, who provide feedback regarding instrumentation, study findings, and draft reports, are expanding.

An important example of the critical role that family members can play is provided by Koroloff and Friesen (1997) in their tests of family members as research associates and linkers to services for youth and families in need. In a test of an intervention focused on increasing access to child mental health services for low-income youth and their families, a family associate model was examined. The family associate was a parent, without formal mental health training, who provided information, support, linkage to resources, and direct assistance, such as help with transportation and child care (Koroloff et al., 1994).

Collaboration with Providers

Weisz and colleagues (1992, 2000) have described important differences between mental health researchers who examine services within tightly controlled clinical trials and those who provide services within real-world settings. There is increasing recognition that if evidence-based services are to be used in real-world settings, then providers must be capable of delivering them within the constraints of their agencies' policies and procedures. Therefore, the core assumption is that when service delivery strategies are being developed, providers need to participate in that development to increase chances of transportability.

However, collaboration with providers in research studies can be complicated. For example, providers may not lack research training and may not appreciate research, thus creating obstacles to collaboration. Further, when research and service programs are brought together, there may be inherent differences in values that need to be dealt with prior to collaborative partnerships moving forward. Finally, for many provider staff, research activities may raise fears. Trust between research staff and providers is also a common issue. Providers may feel protective of clients and question competency and sensitivity of researchers. For example, concerns may be raised that research activities will interfere with the clinical relationship or that clients may experience anxiety or discomfort as a result of participating in research interviews (Lundy et al., 1997). Given the obstacles to collaborating with providers, the same amounts of time, communication, and trust building needed with other community partners to occur in order to effect productive research collaboration.

System-Level Collaboration

Four factors have been identified as contributing to agency involvement in research studies (Mutschler, 1984). First, the relevance of the research to the client population's needs and the workers' job responsibilities has been described as critical to achieving agency "buy-in" in research projects. Next, perceptions of the usefulness of the research outcome to the scope and mission of the agency appear critical to developing a collaborative research agenda with a child mental health organization. Third, involvement of practitioners in the design and implementation of evaluation has been linked with collaborative success. Finally, features of the organization itself, such as availability of computers and the financial commitment to put the results into action, are described as necessary conditions for collaborative research investment for agency personnel. Therefore, as university-based researchers approach child mental health serving agencies, these four factors might be assessed and discussed during the early stages of collaboration.

Collaboration with Communities

Collaborative efforts with communities on behalf of children have been described as resting on three processes that should be taken into consideration. First, key to engaging communities in collaborative research efforts is defining the community and then reaching out to community representatives. Next, there must be a recognition that tensions will arise among collaborative participants depending upon their orientation to service versus research versus the larger community's well-being. Finally, the often-significant cultural differences both within the community and between the community and the university must be considered (Cook, Goeppinger, Brunk, & Price, 1988; Galbraith et al., 1996).

There are many examples of university-based researchers engaging communities on behalf of children (Kellam et al., 2000). In addition, there are recent attempts to specify collaborative mechanisms that can possibly advance the research efforts. For example, research is beginning to be conducted on community advisory and collaborative boards in child-focused research efforts (Madison et al., in press; McKay et al., 2000). More specifically, a collaborative board is a forum for organizing key stakeholders of a specific community and offers the opportunity to formalize the community's involvement in the research efforts. These boards can oversee the development of a research agenda or the implementation of specific research projects. Figure 2.4 models one conceptualization of the collaborative process and the tasks associated with the progression of work within a collaborative board.

The development of relationships between university-based researchers and community partners is based upon the building of trust. A major task in the initial stage of collaborative board constitution is the establishment of a mission statement that addresses all parties' visions for the collaborative work and serves as a guideline for future work. A sample mission statement currently guiding a test of an urban, family-based preventative intervention in provided in Table 2.2 (Madison et al., in press, for details regarding this study; McKay et al., 2000).

The second stage of collaboration concerns the exchange of information. A major task in this phase of the partnership is the development of a common language that facilitates communication between university and community partners. For community members, immersion in the project helps further their understanding of the research, while for university members, immersion in the community aids in their understanding of the context of the work. The third stage of partnership involves shared decision making. In this stage, the task is to share influence, such that multiple stakeholders are involved in determining the direction of the work. Organizationally, the use of committees facilitates the sharing of decision making and power. The penultimate stage of university–community collaborative partnerships concerns leadership development. The main tasks for leadership development are identifying the skills needed to manage the intervention and explicitly enhancing those skills in community members through mentoring and training. The tasks involved at the final phase of partnership—transfer of ownership—include expanding the community base of leadership, transferring all major roles to community members, establishing a community "home," and solidifying university partners' roles as consultants (Madison et al., in press). Both university-based researchers and community partners work actively throughout these stages to foster collaborative relationships and negotiate key tasks of the partnership.

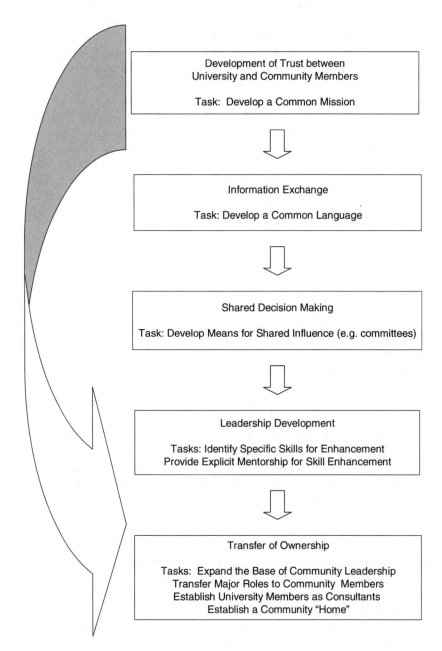

Figure 2.4 A model of the development of collaborative partnerships: stages and tasks.

Table 2.2 Family Program Mission Statement

---

1) We are committed to preventing families and children from getting HIV/AIDS.
2) We will not exploit communities in the process. We are doing research with and for communities, not to communities.
3) We want to increase communities' understanding of how research can be used against them so that they can protect themselves.
4) We want to increase communities' understanding of the strengths within their communities.
5) If a community likes the program, the research staff will help the community find ways to continue the program on its own.
6) We want to increase employment within communities by using programmatic resources in communities wherever possible.
7) We want to explore the possibility of starting programs at earlier ages.

For further information, see Madison et al., in press; McKay et al., 2000.

SUMMARY AND CONCLUSION

The continued presence of a substantial portion of youth experiencing significant mental health issues calls for new models of child mental health services research that address these needs. Further, the development of relevant and effective services has proceeded slowly in response to the serious needs of children. Collaborative research efforts hold promise for addressing these issues as they bring together university-based researchers who have substantial expertise, knowledge of the literature, and access to resources with mental health stakeholders who bring strong commitment to the mental health of youth, expertise related to the needs of youth and their families, and an understanding of the practical realities of agency settings and communities.

There are multiple ways to consider collaboration within the field of child mental health services research. In this chapter, there has been a focus on core collaborative principles that could serve to guide services researchers. In addition, opportunities for increasing collaboration across the research process at varying degrees of depth are presented for the services researcher to consider. Further, examples with different mental health constituents, consumers, families, providers, systems representatives, and communities are offered as possibilities for increasing collaboration within child mental health services research projects.

Although opportunities to collaborate more intensely are available to researchers, these collaborative efforts are not without a specific set of challenges. Collaborative research efforts are labor intensive for both the university-based researcher and the mental health stakeholders. Further, they require a level of communication and sharing of power that has not necessarily been a part of the majority of research projects previously. However, given the great need to develop new ways to serve our nation's youth and the likelihood that services will fail if they do not involve service providers collaboratively the utility of these new approaches to collaboration must be tested (Aponte, Zarski, Bixenstine, & Cibik, 1991; Boyd-Franklin, 1993; Fullilove & Fullilove, 1993).

We know from prior research that the potential effectiveness of child mental health services is limited when those services have not been designed and implemented in ways that acknowledge stressors, scarce contextual resources, target groups' core values, and the skills and capabilities of real-world providers (Boyd-Franklin, 1993; Jensen et al., 1999; McLoyd, 1990). The establishment of strong partnerships is critical to ensuring that effective child mental health services are well received within community-based settings and that innovative programs can be sustained once research funding has ended (Galbraith et al., 1996).

References

Aponte, H. J., Zarski, J. J., Bixenstine, C., & Cibik, P. (1991). Home/community-based services: A two-tier approach. *American Journal of Orthopsychiatry, 61*(3), 403–408.

Armstrong, M. I., & Evans, M. E. (1992). Three intensive community-based programs for children and youth with serious emotional disturbance and their families. *Journal of Child & Family Studies, 1*(1), 61–74.

Arnold L.E., Abikoff, H.B., Cantwell, D.P., Conners, C.K., Elliott, G., Greenhill, L. L., Hechtman, L., Hinshaw, S.P., Hoza, B., Jensen, P.S., Kraemer, H.C., March , J.S., Newcorn, J.H., Pelham, W.E., Richters, J.E., Schiller, E., Severe, J.B., Swanson, J.M., Vereen, D., & Wells, K.C. (1997). National Institute of Mental Health collaborative multimodal treatment study of children with ADHD (the MTA): Design challenges and choices. *Archives of General Psychiatry, 54*, 865–870.

Atkins, M. S, McKay, M., M., Arvanitis, P., London, L., Madison, S., Costigan, C., Haney, P., Zevenbergen, A., Hess, L., Bennett, D., & Webster, D. (1998). An ecological model for school-based mental health services for urban low-income aggressive children. *Journal of Behavioral Health Services & Research, 25*(1), 64–75.

Boyd-Franklin, N. (1993). Racism, secret-keeping, and African-American families. In E. Imber-Black (Ed.), *Secrets in families and family therapy* (pp. 331–354). New York, Norton.

Brandenberg, N. A., Friedman, R. M., & Silver, S. E. (1987). The epidemiology of childhood psychiatric disorders: Prevalence findings from recent studies. *Journal of the American Academy of Child and Adolescent Psychiatry, 29*, 76–83.

Brent, D. A., Bridge, J., Johnson, B. A., & Connolly, J. (1998). Suicidal behavior runs in families: A controlled family study of adolescent suicide victims. In R. J. Kosky & H. S. Eshkevari (Eds.), *Suicide prevention: The global context* (pp. 51–65). New York: Plenum Press.

Brent, D. A., Kolko, D. J., Birmaher, B., Baugher, M., Bridge, J., Roth, C., & Holder, D. (1998). Predictors of treatment efficacy in a clinical trial of three psychosocial treatments for adolescent depression. *Journal of the American Academy of Child & Adolescent Psychiatry, 37*(9), 906–914.

Burns, B.J., Costello, E.J., Angold, A., Tweed, D., Stangle, D., & Farmer, E.H.Z. (1995). Children's mental health service use across service sectors. *Health Affairs, 124*, 147–159.

Callahan, K., Rademacher, J. A., Hildreth, B. L., & Hildreth, B. L. (1998). The effect of parent participation in strategies to improve the homework performance of students who are at risk. *RASE: Remedial & Special Education, 19*(3), 131–141.

Catalano, R. F., Arthur, M. W., Hawkins, D. J., Berglund, L., & Olson, J. J. (1998). Comprehensive community- and school-based interventions to prevent antisocial behavior. In R. Loeber & D. P. Farrington (Eds), *Serious and violent juvenile offenders: Risk factors and successful interventions* (pp. 248–283). Thousand Oaks, CA: Sage.

Catron, T., Harris, V. S., & Weiss, B. (1998). Posttreatment results after 2 years of services in the Vanderbilt school-based counseling project. In M. H. Epstein & K. Kutash (Eds.), *Outcomes for children and youth with emotional and behavioral disorders and their families: Programs and evaluation best practices* (pp. 633–656). Austin, TX: PROED.

Collins, B., & Collins, T. (1990). Parent/professional relationships in the treatment of seriously emotionally disturbed children and adolescents. *Social Work, 35*(6), 522–527.

Cook, H. L., Goeppinger, L., Brunk, S. E., & Price, L. L. (1988). A reexamination of community participation in health: Lessons from three community health projects. *Family & Community Health, 11*(2), 1–13.

DeChillo, N. (1993). Collaboration between social workers and families of patients with mental illness. *Families in Society, 74*(2), 104–115.

Dixon, L. (2000). Assertive community treatment: Twenty-five years of gold. *Psychiatric Services, 51*(6), 759–765.

Elliott, D., Koroloff, N., Koren, P., & Friesen, B. (1998). Improving access to children's mental health services: The family associate approach. In M. Epstein & K. Kutash (Eds.), *Outcomes for children and youth with emotional and behavioral disorders and their families: Programs and evaluation best practices* (pp. 581–609). Austin, TX: PROED.

Evans, M. E, Armstrong, M. I., Thompson, F., & Lee, L. K. (1994). Assessing the outcomes of parent- and provider-designed systems of care for children with emotional and behavioral disorders. *Psychiatric Quarterly, 65*(4), 257–272.

Franco, L, Chambers, N., Miranda, A., McKay, M. & CHAMP Collaborative Board in New York (2006). "Voices from the community: Key ingredients for community collaboration." *Social Work in Mental Health,* 5 (3/4), 307–325. Also published in: (2007) in M. McKay & R. Paikoff (Eds.), *Community Collaborative Partnerships: The Foundation for HIV Prevention Research Efforts.* New York: Haworth Press.

Friedman, R. (1996). The Fort Bragg study: What can we conclude? *Journal of Child & Family Studies, 5*(2), 161–168.

Friend, M., & Cook, L. (1990). Collaboration as a predictor for success in school reform. *Journal of Educational & Psychological Consultation, 1*(1), 69–86.

Fullilove, M. T., & Fullilove, R. E. III. (1993). Understanding sexual behaviors and drug use among African-Americans: A case study of issues for survey research. In D. G. Ostrow & R. C. Kessler (Eds.). *Methodological issues in AIDS behavioral research* (pp. 117–132). New York: Plenum Press.

Galbraith, L., Ricardo, I., Stanton, B., & Black, M. (1996). Challenges and rewards of involving community in research: An overview of the "Focus on Kids" HIV risk reduction program. *Health Education Quarterly, 23*(3), 383–394.

Gasch, R., Poulson, D. M., Fullilove, R. E., & Fullilove, M. T. (1991). Shaping AIDS education and prevention programs for African Americans amidst community decline. *Journal of Negro Education, 60*(1), 85–96.

Hatch, L., Moss, N., Saran, A., & Presley-Cantrell, L. (1993). Community research: Partnership in Black communities. *American Journal of Preventive Medicine, 9*(6, Suppl.), 27–31.

Henggeler, S. W. (1999). Multisystemic therapy: An overview of clinical procedures, outcomes, and policy implications. *Child Psychology & Psychiatry Review, 4*(1), 2–10.

Henggeler, S. W, Cunningham, P. B., Pickrel, S. G., & Schoenwald, S. K. (1996). Multisystemic therapy: An effective violence prevention approach for serious juvenile offenders. *Journal of Adolescence, 19*(1), 47–61.

Henggeler, S. W., Schoenwald, S. K., & Pickrel, S. G. (1995). Multisystemic therapy: Bridging the gap between university- and community-based treatment. *Journal of Consulting & Clinical Psychology, 63*(5), 709–717.

Hibbs, E., & Jensen, P. (1996). *Psychosocial treatments for child and adolescent disorders: Empirically based strategies for clinical practice.* Washington, DC: American Psychological Association.

Hoagwood, K., Burns, B.J., Kiser, L., Ringeisen, H. & Schoenwald, S. (2001). Evidence-based practices in child and adolescent mental health services. *Psychiatric Services, 52*(9), 1079–1089.

Hooper-Briar, K., & Lawson, H. (1994). *Serving children, youth and families through interprofessional collaboration and service integration: A framework for action.* Oxford, OH: The Danforth Foundation & The Institute for Educational Renewal at Miami University.

Horkheimer, M., & Adorno, T. (1972). Dialect of Enlightenment (John Cumming, Trans). New York: Continuum Publishing. (Original work published 1944).

Institute of Medicine. (1989). *Biomedical and behavioral research scientists: Their training and supply.* Washington, DC: National Academy Press.

Israel, B. A., Schulz, A. L., Parker, E. A., & Becker, A. B. (1998). Review of community based research: Assessing partnership approaches to improve public health. *Annual Review of Public Health, 19,* 173–202.

Jensen, P. S. (2000). Links among theory, research, and practice: Cornerstones of clinical collaboration in child mental health services research. *Journal of Clinical Child Psychology, 28*(4), 553–557.

Jensen, P. S., Hoagwood, K., & Trickett, E. L. (1999). Ivory towers or earthen trenches? Community collaborations to foster real-world research. *Applied Developmental Science, 1*(4), 206–212.

Jivanjee, P., & Friesen, B. (1997). Shared expertise: Family participation in interprofessional training. *Journal of Emotional & Behavioral Disorders, 5*(4), 205–211.

Kazdin, A. E. (1993). Adolescent mental health: Prevention and treatment programs. *American Psychologist, 48*(2), 127–141.

Kelleher, K. L. (1999). Pediatric psychologist as investigator in primary care. *Journal of Pediatric Psychology, 24*(5), 459–462.

Knitzer, J. (1989). Children's mental health: The advocacy challenge "and miles to go before we sleep." In R. M. Friedman & A. L. Duchnowski (Eds.), *Advocacy on behalf of children with serious emotional problems* (pp. 15–27). Springfield, IL: Charles C. Thomas.

Knitzer, L. (1982). Children's rights in the family and society: Dilemmas and realities. *American Journal of Orthopsychiatry, 52*(3), 481–495.

Kellam, S. (2000). Community and institutional partnerships for school violence prevention. *Preventing School Violence: Plenary Papers of the 1999 Conference on Criminal Justice Research and evaluation—Enhancing Policy and Practice Through Research, Volume 2* (pp. 1–21). Washington, DC: National Institute of Justice.

Knitzner, L. (1996). Children's mental health: Changing paradigms and policies. In E. F. Zigler & S. L. Kagan (Eds.), *Children, families, and government: Preparing for the twenty-first century* (pp. 207–232). New York: Cambridge University Press.

Knitzner, L. (2000). Early childhood mental health services: A policy and systems development perspective. In L. P. Shonkoff & S. L. Meisels (Eds.), *Handbook of early childhood intervention* (2nd edition) (pp. 416–438). New York: Cambridge University Press.

Koroloff, N. M., Elliott, D. J., Koren, P. E., and Friesen, B. J. (1994). Connecting low-income families to mental health services: The role of the family associate. *Journal of Emotional & Behavioral Disorders, 2*(4), 240–246.

Koroloff, N. M., & Friesen, B. L. (1997). Challenges in conducting family-centered mental health services research. *Journal of Emotional & Behavioral Disorders, 5*(3), 130–137.

Krauss, B. J. (1998). HIV education for teens and preteens in a high-prevalence inner-city neighborhood. *Families in Society, 78*(6), 579–591.

Labonte, R. (1994). Health promotion and empowerment: Reflections on professional practice. *Health Education Quarterly, 21*(2), 253–268.

Lehman, A. F., Dixon, L., Hoch, L. S., DeForge, B., Kernan, E., & Frank, R. (1999). Cost-effectiveness of assertive community treatment for homeless persons with severe mental illness. *British Journal of Psychiatry, 174*, 346–352.

Lundy, A., Gottheil, E., McLellan, A., Weinstein, S., Sterling, R., & Serrota, R. (1997). Underreporting of cocaine use at posttreatment follow-up and the measurement of treatment effectiveness. *Journal of Nervous & Mental Disease, 185*(7), 459–462.

Madison, S., Bell, C., Sewell, S., Nash, G., McKay, M. M., & Paikoff, R. (in press). True community/academic partnerships. *Psychiatric Services.*

Madison, S. M., McKay, M. M., Paikoff, R, & Bell, C. C. (2000). Basic research and community collaboration: Necessary ingredients for the development of a family-based HIV prevention program. *AIDS Education & Prevention, 12*(4), 281–298.

McCabe, K., Yeh, M., Hough, R. L., Landsverk, L., Hurlburt, M. S., Culver, S. W., & Reynolds, B. (1999). Racial/ethnic representation across five public sectors of care for youth. *Journal of Emotional & Behavioral Disorders, 7*(2), 72–82.

McCormick, A., McKay, M. M., Wilson, M., McKinney, L., Paikoff, R, Bell, C., Baptiste, D., Coleman, D., Gillming, G., Madison, S., & Scott, R. (2000). Involving families in an urban HIV preventive intervention: How community collaboration addresses barriers to participation. *AIDS Education & Prevention, 12*(4), 299–307.

McKay, M. M., Baptiste, D., Coleman, D., Madison, S., McKinney, L., Paikoff, R., & CHAMP Collaborative Board. (2000). Preventing HIV risk exposure in urban communities: The CHAMP Family Program. In W. Pequegnat & J. Szapocznik (Eds.), *Working with families in the era of HIV/AIDS* (pp. 67–87). Thousand Oaks, CA: Sage.

McKay, M. M., Gonzales, L., Quintana, E., Kim, L., & Abdul-Adil, L. (1999). Multiple family groups: An alternative for reducing disruptive behavioral difficulties of urban children. *Research on Social Work Practice, 9*(5), 593–607.

McKay, M. M., McCadam, K., & Gonzales, L. L. (1996). Addressing the barriers to mental health services for inner city children and their caretakers. *Community Mental Health Journal, 32*(4,) 353–361.

McKay, M. M., McCadam, K, & Gonzales, L. (1997). Addressing the barriers to mental health services for inner-city children and their caretakers. *Community Mental Health Journal, 32*(4), 353–361.

McKay, M. M., Stoewe, L., McCadam, K., & Gonzales, L. (1998). Increasing access to child mental health services for urban children and their caregivers. *Health & Social Work, 23*(1), 9–15.

McLoyd, V. C. (1990). The impact of economic hardship on Black families and children: Psychological distress, parenting, and socioemotional development. *Child Development, 61*(2), 311–346.

Murray C., & Lopez A.D. (1996). *The Global Burden of Disease: A Comprehensive Assessment of Mortality and Disability from Disease, Injuries, and Risk Factors in 1990 and Projected to 2020.* Boston, MA: The Harvard School of Public Health on behalf of the World Health Organization and The World Bank.

Mutschler, E. (1984). Evaluating Practice: A Study of Research Utilization by Practitioners. *Social work, 29*(4), 332–337.

Pickett, S. A., Heller, T., & Cook, L. A. (1998). Professional-led versus family-led support groups: Exploring the differences. *Journal of Behavioral Health Services & Research, 25*(4), 437–445.

Paikoff, R. L., Parfenoff, S. H., Williams, S. A., & McCormick, A. (1997). Parenting, parent-child relationships, and sexual possibility situations among urban African American preadolescents: Preliminary findings and implications for HIV prevention. *Journal of Family Psychology, 11*(1), 11–22.

Pickett-Schenk, S. A., Cook, L. A, & Laris, A. (2000). Journey of Hope program outcomes. *Community Mental Health Journal, 36*(4), 413–424.

Reed, G., & Collins, B. (1994). Mental health research and service delivery: A three communities model. *Psychosocial Rehabilitation Journal, 17*(4), 69–81.

Roe, K., Minkler, M., & Saunders, F. (1995). Combining research, advocacy, and education: The methods of the Grandparent Caregiver Study. *Health Education Quarterly, 22*(4), 458–475.

Rogers, E. S., & Palmer-Erbs, V. (1994). Participatory action research: Implications for research and evaluation in psychiatric rehabilitation. *Psychosocial Rehabilitation Journal, 1*(2), 3–12.

Ruffolo, M. C. (1998). Mental health services for children and adolescents. In J. B. Williams & K. Ell (Eds.), *Advances in mental health research: Implications for practice* (pp. 399–419). Washington, D.C.: NASW Press.

Santos, A., Hawkins, G., Julius, B., Deci, P., Hiers, T., & Burns, B. (1993). A pilot study of assertive community treatment for patients with chronic psychotic disorders. *American Journal of Psychiatry, 150*(3), 501–504.

Santos, A., Henggeler, S., Burns, B., Arana, G., & Meisler, N. (1995). Research on field-based services: models for reform in the delivery of mental health care to populations with complex clinical problems. *American Journal of Psychiatry, 152*(8), 1111–1123.

Schorr, L. B. (1989). *Within our reach: Breaking the cycle of disadvantage.* New York: Anchor Books/Doubleday.

Singer, M. (1993). Knowledge for use: Anthropology and community-centered substance abuse research. *Social Science & Medicine, 37*(1), 15–25.

Spergel, L. A., & Grossman, S. F. (1997). The Little Village Project: A community approach to the gang problem. *Social Work, 42*(5), 456–470.

Stevenson, H., & White, L. (1994). AIDS prevention struggles in ethnocultural neighborhoods: Why research partnerships with community based organizations can't wait. *AIDS Education & Prevention, 6*(2), 126–139.

Tolan, P. H., & Henry, D. (1996). Patterns of psychopathology among urban poor children: Comorbidity and aggression effects. *Journal of Consulting & Clinical Psychology, 64*(5), 1094–1099.

Tuma, L. M. (1989). Mental health services for children: The state of the art. *American Psychologist, 44*(2), 188–199.

U.S. Department of Health and Human Services. (2000). *Mental health: A report of the Surgeon General.* Washington, DC: U.S. Department of Health and Human Services.

Vitiello, B., & Jensen, P. (1997). Medication development and testing in children and adolescents: Current problems, future directions. *Archives of General Psychiatry, 54*(9), 871–876.

Weisz, L. R. (2000). Agenda for child and adolescent psychotherapy research: On the need to put science into practice. *Archives of General Psychiatry, 57*(9), 837–838.

Weisz, L. R., Donenberg, G. R., Han, S. S., & Weiss, B. (1995). Bridging the gap between laboratory and clinic in child and adolescent psychotherapy. *Journal of Consulting & Clinical Psychology, 63*(5), 688–701.

Weisz, L. R., & Hawley, K. M. (1998). Finding, evaluating, refining, and applying empirically supported treatments for children and adolescents. *Journal of Clinical Child Psychology, 27*(2), 206–216.

Weisz, L. R, Hawley, K. M., Pilkonis, P. A, Woody, S. R., & Follette, W. C. (2000). Stressing the (other) three Rs in the search for empirically supported treatments: Review procedures, research quality, relevance to practice and the public interest. *Clinical Psychology: Science & Practice, 7*(3), 243–258.

Weisz, L. R., Weiss, B., & Donenberg, G. R. (1992). The lab versus the clinic: Effects of child and adolescent psychotherapy. *American Psychologist, 47*(12), 1578–1585.

Wood, D., & Gray, B. (1991). Toward a comprehensive theory of collaboration. *Journal of Applied Behavioral Science, 27*(2), 139–167.

Chapter Three

Under New Management: Research Collaboration with Family Members and Youth

Nancy Koroloff, Trina Osher, Pauline Jivanjee, Michael D. Pullmann, Kathryn Sofich, Leanne Guthrie, Jane Adams, and Shalene Murphy

This chapter describes some ways that families who care for children with mental, emotional, or behavioral problems, youth who are served by the children's mental health system, and researchers have collaborated in research and evaluation. This chapter exemplifies collaboration in its fullest form. Different authors wrote separate parts of the chapter and then edited others' sections. Editing another's written work is an act of some intimacy, and to a great extent this collaboration was possible because the authors had worked together before and trusted each other. Readers will be aware of changes in written voice as they proceed through this chapter. As a group we decided to keep the different writing styles rather than edit the chapter to read as if one person wrote it. Collaborative research is somewhat like this chapter; in the end, the results reflect the expertise contributed by the individuals involved and may not coalesce into a single, unified, polished research whole.

Language can shape and sometimes limit collaboration. We struggled to find terms that communicate our belief that everyone on the research team brings ideas, experiences, and expertise that are valuable to the research process. In this chapter, researchers whose expertise comes from academic training will be referred to as academic researchers—although some are not employed by a university. Family members or youth are in some sections called just that, "family members" or "youth," and in other sections "family researchers," "youth researchers," or "family evaluators." The difference among these terms lies in the prominence of the researcher role in the family or youth's life. When the family member is employed in a research position that occupies a major part of their work life (e.g., Clark County, Washington), attaching the researcher label seems appropriate. In other cases, when the family member or youth's role in research is a small part of their multifaceted lives, the researcher label was thought to be an overrepresentation.

HISTORICAL DEVELOPMENT OF CONSUMER INVOLVEMENT IN MENTAL HEALTH RESEARCH

The involvement of family members, youth, and adult consumers has roots in the expanding sociopolitical consciousness of the country that emerged in the 1960s out of the unrest created by poverty, racism, and unmet social needs. The increasing public demand for citizen involvement was a reaction to a widely held concern about the inability of publicly sponsored programs to respond to the needs of communities, particularly poor and minority communities. At that time, suspicion of government and bureaucracy was high, and "citizen participation" was considered a possible antidote.

Through the efforts of advocates, consumer groups, and committed policy makers, a series of legislative acts moved the country toward more democratic, grassroots control of the shape of public programs. Public health sponsored some of the first legislation that incorporated the voice of consumers into program governance, emphasized consumer involvement in health planning, and defined consumers as individuals who lived in the geographic area served and used the local health care (Checkoway, 1979; Koseki, 1977). Three types of federal social programs (urban renewal, antipoverty programs, and the Model Cities programs) required varying degrees of citizen participation and control. In these programs, "citizen" was defined to include those individuals who lived in the communities affected by the project. At the time, Arnstein (1969) noted that "citizen participation is a little like eating spinach: no one is against it in principle because it is good for you" (p. 216). She articulated the "ladder of participation," which ranged from manipulation and therapy (at the bottom of the ladder) to designated power and citizen control at the top.

One of the first concrete steps toward consumer and/or family member involvement in mental health is found in the 1975 amendments to the Community Mental Health Centers Act of 1963, which required that residents of the catchment area be represented on the center's advisory board and involved in evaluation of center services (Pinto & Fiester, 1979). The legislation clearly specified that "the participating citizens must include broad representation of all elements of the community such as professionals, lay persons, appropriate consumers ...." (Windle & Cibulka, 1981, p. 7). The general belief at that time was that most consumers were unsuitable to participate in the developing mental health movement because of their bias for or against a particular agency or service and that many were incapable of knowing what they needed or wanted (Chu & Trotter, 1974).

Another stream of sociopolitical activity that advanced the acceptance of family members and adult consumers as equal collaborators emerged from the independent living movement of the early 1970s. Leaders of this movement demanded greater participation of individuals with disabilities in a variety of areas, including greater control over research on rehabilitation (DeJong, 1979; Santelli, Ginsberg, Sullivan, & Niederhauser, 2002). By the early 1990s rehabilitation research had moved toward full participation of consumers in the research process under the theoretical auspices of participatory action research (PAR). By 1993, the National Institute on Disability and Rehabilitation Research (NIDRR) had endorsed full participation of all constituency groups in research and the incorporation of PAR into all NIDRR activities (Rogers & Palmer-Erbs, 1994). Participatory action research developed out of the tradition of action research and is based in the belief that oppressed people should be fully engaged in the process of investigation. It is connected to social action and social movements "as a way for researchers and oppressed people to join in solidarity to take collective action, both short and long term, for radical social change" (Hall, 1993, p. xiv).

Turnbull, Friesen, and Ramirez (1998) offer a much-quoted description of PAR as "a process whereby the researchers and stakeholders (those who potentially benefit from research results) collaborate in the design and all phases...of the research process" (p. 178). They further assert that PAR's intended outcome is to change the situations or problems that are implied by the original research questions. The National Institute on Disability and Rehabilitation Research defined families and youth as stakeholders in the research process and this influenced many researchers whose studies of services for children with disabilities were funded through NIDRR. In concert with the policy shift toward PAR, the two research and training centers (RTCs) related to children's mental health (jointly funded by NIDRR and the Center for Mental Health Services) incorporated its tenets into their research activities. Although already recognized for the ways in which they involved family members in their projects, both RTCs found the increased attention to PAR provided renewed impetus and support for collaborating with family members on research projects.

The most recent segment of the legislative trail toward collaboration in research is the Comprehensive Community Mental Health Services for Children with Serious Emotional Disturbances Act of 1992 and its amendments. This act supports the Comprehensive Community Mental Health Services for Children and their Families Program, which in 1993 began funding states, communities, territories, and native American tribes to improve community-based systems of care to meet the needs of children with emotional, mental, and behavior disorders. A major emphasis of this program is partnerships with families in all aspects of the service system, resulting in an emerging collaboration with family members in the evaluation of funded systems of care. Research demonstrates that this emphasis is working. In 1998, Osher, Van Kammen, and Zaro (2001) conducted a survey of 22 funded sites, asking three partners in each site (site director, evaluator, family leader) about the involvement of family members in the national and local evaluation required of each site. Seventy percent of respondents reported that family members were involved in modification of instruments to make them more relevant, and about half reported that families were involved in collecting data and in its analysis. Eighty-two percent of the site directors reported that families were involved in the review and utilization of data. The authors concluded that, although participation varied from site to site, families were performing a wide range of roles within the evaluation team and most were being compensated for this work.

At this point in the evolution of mental health research, there are two ends of the collaboration continuum involving academic researchers and family members/youth researchers (Turnbull et al., 1998). At one end and most common, the academic researcher maintains control of the research questions and is the major decision maker regarding research design and data collection protocols. Family members participate in the discussion, review the instruments, collect data, help to analyze and interpret the data, and help to disseminate it. The family members may have extraordinary influence, but ultimately the academic researcher makes the final decision. This division of labor is often seen in the evaluation of federally funded programs, especially those with cross-site evaluation requirements. It is described in the following case study of Clark County, Washington, where family members have substantial influence, and consequently the data collection process as well as the depth and quality of data are affected, as are the strategies for dissemination and utilization. The research questions and design in this case study were largely predetermined by academic researchers on the national evaluation team.

At the other end of the continuum, family members or youth are the "principal investigators" for the research and the academic researcher is a consultant. In this approach, family members or youth determine the research questions and design with input from the academic researcher. This shift in power affects the resulting research topic as well as the way data are collected and disseminated. Fewer examples of this approach are available, probably because it is newer, it does not have the tradition and momentum of academically driven research, family organizations often do not have a research infrastructure, and because funding sources are not yet convinced of its utility (Maclure, 1990; Rogers & Palmer-Erbs, 1994). However, there are examples available—the sections describing the Family-Driven Research Study and the Youth-Driven Research Project depict this approach.

The final section of this chapter describes the experiences and perspectives of academic researchers who have conducted collaborative research in partnership with family members and youth. Based on data from a qualitative study conducted at the Research and Training Center on Family Support and Children's Mental Health in Portland, Oregon, this section provides an expanded understanding of the benefits and challenges of collaborative research through the eyes of the researcher partner. Tables 1, 2 and 3 describe the roles and functions of researchers and families in forging collaborations, as well as tips for co-creating studies that are relevant to family perspectives and to scientific advancement.

Table 3.1 Choosing Research Partners: Some Things to Consider

- ☐ Do they share your values around families and family involvement?
- ☐ Are they comfortable with families taking the lead in research?
- ☐ Will they provide technical assistance and not take over?
- ☐ Do they care about the subject matter?
- ☐ Do they practice participatory research in the field?
- ☐ Do they have the necessary expertise?
- ☐ What resources can they bring to the project—such as other researchers with different areas of expertise?
- ☐ Who do they work for or with?
- ☐ Are they affiliated with a university?
- ☐ Are they in it for the long haul?

Table 3.2 Tips for Getting Started

For Researchers	For Families
☐ Talk to other researchers who have been in this role before. Read the literature on participatory research.	☐ Choose researchers who care about the subject matter and have expertise in the area.
☐ Do not expect the study to be too well defined at first. Listen to why the study is important to the family members.	☐ Be patient. Planning a research project will undoubtedly take longer than you anticipate.
☐ Discuss the role that you will play on the study with the family members.	☐ Let researchers know what you expect and need from them. Be honest about your own limitations.
☐ Make a list of questions that can help you understand what the families are interested in studying.	☐ Start with a sense of what you want to study and what your research questions might be.
☐ Identify the resources you can bring to this effort.	☐ Identify where you may find financial support for the study.
☐ Think about the strengths that you as an individual bring to this effort.	

Table 3.3 Tips for Doing the Study

For Researchers	For Families
☐ Learn to be an advocate for the perspective of the family members. Challenge yourself to think of ways to keep the work rigorous without giving up the family perspective.	☐ Be prepared to stretch and try things you have not tried before.
☐ Educate family members about research and evaluation, specifically, as they are ready to use the information.	☐ Before going too far in the project, make sure to get grounded in basic research language and concepts.
☐ Help translate the language of research and evaluation for family members.	☐ Start speaking the language or research to each other early.
☐ Help family members craft materials that are scientifically rigorous and family friendly.	☐ Become educated on institutional review board requirements and procedures and make them work for the reasons they exist: to protect human subjects, something we all value.
☐ Be patient. There is more processing and teamwork when working with family groups than you may be accustomed to.	☐ Do not be afraid to ask questions or make mistakes.
☐ Listen for what this will tell you about what else they need to learn about research or where to go next with the study.	☐ Be clear in describing when you want researchers to follow and when you want them to lead.
☐ Learn to listen. Let family members educate you about family and child issues.	☐ Keep an open mind about every aspect of the study. Be prepared for findings that are surprising or do not conform to your own views and biases.

☐ **Appreciate the differences between researchers and family members.**
☐ **Find ways to celebrate milestones and successes along the way.**

CLARK COUNTY, WASHINGTON—CHILDREN'S MENTAL HEALTH SYSTEM OF CARE

Three major characteristics of the Clark County system of care evaluation led to successful collaboration between family member evaluators and academically trained researchers. First, Clark County has some extremely dedicated family members who are committed to advocating for their children and their community and are interested in being involved in system-of-care efforts at all levels. Second, the group contracted to work on this evaluation, the Regional Research Institute for Human Services at Portland State University (RRI), is at the forefront of the consumer as researcher movement. (The authors of this chapter are researchers at the RRI. Research published by members of the RRI in this area include, among others: Elliott, Koroloff, Koren, & Friesen, 1998; Koroloff & Friesen, 1997; Koroloff, Friesen, Reilly, & Rinkin, 1996; Turnbull, Friesen, & Ramirez, 1998.) Third, in 1998 Clark County was a recipient of a Comprehensive Community Mental Health for Children and their Families Initiative grant. A requirement of this grant is employing family members of children with serious emotional disorders. This required the county administrators and providers, who did not necessarily have experience supporting families in professional roles, to adjust their practice.

Toward the end of the first (planning) year of the grant, the RRI contracted with the local family support organization to provide one of their employees as a core member of the evaluation team. Paula Savage, a single mother of three children, including a 14-year-old child and a 7-year-old child with emotional and behavioral disorders, was incorporated into the evaluation team at several levels. In the first collaborative project, she and her oldest child heavily revised the draft version of the consent forms to make them more family friendly, while researchers on the team ensured the inclusion of the necessary ethical and legal content. Paula acknowledged being confused at first while she learned the language of evaluation and how to communicate with researchers. But she was impressed by the significance of the collaboration, "I felt like my family's experience was of value, that I was more than a token parent. When working with some professionals, there have been times when I felt like our experiences were meaningless."

As part of the research team, Paula strongly advocated for her ideas and beliefs. Not satisfied with available instruments for examining wraparound team meetings, she took the lead in developing one. To do this, she used a variety of resources available in the RRI's research library on scale development, and she used information she had accumulated while attending wraparound facilitator trainings. The resulting instrument was reviewed by the entire evaluation team and incorporated into the evaluation protocol. She also added significant family voice to the hiring and training of family information specialists (research interviewers). Some of the interviewers were also caregivers of children with emotional and behavioral disorders.

Collaboration between families and researchers in Clark County has faced many of the challenges and benefits discussed by others (Allen & Stefanowski-Hudd, 1987; Koroloff & Friesen, 1997; McKay, Chapter Two, this volume), including the difficulty in reconciling the separate goals of traditional research and family-driven research, respecting the skills and experience of various partners, and resolving real or perceived conflicts of interest. These difficulties often parallel the hotly contested debates in the "paradigm wars" between positivist and constructivist approaches to research. For instance, a major argument of positivist opponents of collaboration between family advocates and traditional researchers is the issue of "blurred boundaries" and all of its related challenges (conflicts of interest, co-opting, perceived lack of objectivity in family members, perceived lack of rigor in researchers). However, with proper safeguards for truthfulness in research, a constructivist approach views "blurred boundaries" as "spanned boundaries," or an opportunity to discover points of view previously unavailable to academic researchers.

In Clark County, researchers have benefited from collaboration with families as evaluators for several reasons: the information gathered from families is believed to be more accurate; families have access to a social world that academicians may not; family members' interpretation of research findings helps provide realistic view of the data; and family members may add respect or credibility to the research results in the eyes of advocates. These benefits are a direct result of a family evaluator's ability to connect two worlds. Likewise, families benefit from collaboration with researchers for several reasons: the research is more likely to explore areas that are of interest to family advocates; the results are more likely to be disseminated to families; and being part of the research team may add respect or credibility to families' beliefs in the eyes of providers.

A traditional objection to hiring families as evaluators and interviewers is that they may lack the objectivity necessary for rigorous research, and that their own opinions and experience may skew the responses from participants in the study. This objection stems from the fear of blurred boundaries between the roles of researcher and advocate. It is true that research has thoroughly documented social desirability bias and interviewer bias, wherein aspects of the interviewer affect the responses of participants (Nancarrow & Brace, 2000; Shaughnessy & Zechmeister, 1990). Participants may respond in ways they believe the interviewers want them to respond, or the interviewer may lead participants into certain responses because of the interviewer's own bias.

Researchers trained in traditional, positivist methods are taught to reduce these biases by hiring the most objective interviewers as possible. In actual practice, this means hiring interviewers that are the most similar to *the researchers* as possible—usually university students from upper-middle class families. Why students, who carry their own assumptions (possibly including blame and prejudice because of a lack of adequate or real-life experience with children that have mental health problems), are considered more objective is a question left unanswered. On the other hand, based on our experience we believe that it is important to hire interviewers who can build rapport and trust, so they may collect the most accurate, valid information possible while ensuring that participants continue to participate in the study. In this view, and similar to the values and beliefs of constructivist and naturalistic researchers, complete objectivity is considered an unobtainable goal. Instead, participant openness and honesty are deemed achievable through building rapport; for that reason, interviewers should be more similar to *the participants* than the researchers.

This approach may alarm conventionally trained researchers, who may think that scientific rigor will be lost. In our study, we have found that rigor can be maintained through basic safeguards such as proper training, open communication with all members of the evaluation team, family members' understanding of the principles of research, and researchers' understanding of the experiences of family members. It is important for academic researchers to engage in periodic supervision of the interviews, not only to ensure rigor but also so supervisors understand the realities of interviewing. Conversely, it is important for family evaluators to engage in the analysis and interpretation of data, not only to add direct experience to the interpretation but also so they understand the concrete reasons behind scientific rigor. Through collaboration between family members and academic researchers, the research may more effectively represent reality.

Family information specialists in the Clark County evaluation report that they believe that families are more open and honest with them than they would be with an interviewer who lacks the experience of raising a child with mental health problems. "It's different when families I'm interviewing know that I have kids; then they aren't as guarded," said Leanne Guthrie, an interviewer in the evaluation and mother of three, including one child with a behavioral disorder. "It's like they know that I'm not taking their information and judging them. You can see the mistrust melt right off of them." Because of the social stigma of having a child with mental health problems, families that are interviewed may be reluctant to share information with people they feel cannot personally relate to them.

Conversely, this ability to relate with families may be emotionally draining for family evaluators because of strong feelings of empathy. Leanne reported that her empathy is the most difficult part of interviewing because of the desire to help: "With some of the families that I interview, I feel like I can't wait for the research study to be over so I can call them up to help them out. Some of my families could become friends." It is the evaluation team's view that this empathy is essential to building rapport and trust, but that these issues must be constantly discussed and addressed during staff meetings. This is important for the mental health of the interviewer and for the quality of the research. Through proper training, trust between family evaluators and university researchers, open communication about conflicts that arise, and reinforcement of the shared goal of capturing the most accurate information possible, the Clark County evaluation team has addressed real issues of conflict of interest and threats to objectivity. It is our view that the potential bias of family evaluators is exaggerated, especially when the interviewer, the team, and the community continually address the possibility of such bias. "I always have to keep in mind that I have to separate my role of advocacy from my role of researcher," said Paula.

In addition to bringing their skills to interviewing, families as evaluators, because of their experiences and their deep understanding of the issues that face families with children with serious mental health problems, can direct research and analysis to salient concerns. They may also be better able to detect real-world problems in the research methodology, interview structure, or findings. In Clark County, the family evaluators on the research team have helped focus analyses and dissemination on topics different from the usual research focus on youth functioning and services for identified youth. Topics that the Clark County evaluation team has investigated include caregiver strain, family resources, family functioning, and services for caregivers and other family members. Caregivers on the evaluation team were the driving force behind the exploration of these issues.

After the initial examination of the findings, the family evaluators have interpreted the data and fine-tuned the analyses based on their own experiences and the experiences of those they have interviewed. They have noticed problems with the data that required further examination or revealed errors. Paula Savage said that one of the most difficult challenges of the study is that "sometimes it is hard to reconcile what I experience with what the data says." Even after the analysis and interpretation is done, collaboration between family evaluators and university researchers is essential in disseminating the findings in an understandable manner. In dissemination, abstract concepts become clear when family evaluators relate their lives to the research findings.

The evaluation of the Clark County system of care has significantly more family involvement in data collection, analysis, and dissemination than standard mental health research; however, the evaluation is still driven by academic researchers. Academic researchers largely determine the research questions, the data collection instruments and methods, and the audiences for dissemination. Other research, such as the study described in the section below, has taken an alternative approach, where the family members take a leadership role in collaboration with academic researchers.

FAMILY INVOLVEMENT IN SYSTEMS OF CARE: EXAMPLE OF A FAMILY-DRIVEN STUDY

The family-driven study is another example of collaboration with family members in research. However, it differs from the Clark County project in that family members are taking the lead in conducting the research study with the researcher serving as a consultant. This study was conducted under the leadership of the Federation of Families for Children's Mental Health with assistance from the Georgia Parent Support Network and in partnership with ORC Macro International. It was funded by the Child, Adolescent, and Family Branch of the federal Center for Mental Health Services as a component of the National Evaluation of the Comprehensive Mental Health Services for Children and Their Families Program. The study was designed to respond to concerns, expressed by family members of children with mental health needs, that children's mental health research to date has not addressed some of the topics that are important to families. Underlying the study were four key assumptions: *(1)* family members have the capacity to learn and become skilled in evaluation and research activities; *(2)* family members and researchers can enter into full, equal partnerships that are based on trust, respect, and shared goals; *(3)* research can be enhanced by having the family perspective and researcher perspective equally represented during the design and conduct of the study; and *(4)* the results of a study are more likely to be credible, valid, and reliable to other researchers, family members, and the broader field of mental health because of the involvement of family members and researchers.

The family-driven study derived, in part, from two other unique activities. The first was a collaboration between researchers and family members to determine the extent to which family members were involved in the evaluation activities of 22 federally funded system-of-care grantees (Osher, Van Kammen, & Zaro, 2001). The second was the development of a curriculum to train family members to understand and use research and evaluation reports as tools for advocacy (Federation of Families for Children's Mental Health, 2002). The intent of the family-driven study was to apply the family involvement principle of systems of care (Stroul & Friedman, 1986, p. 18) to research by supporting family members and youth as they designed and conducted a research study of some aspect of families' experiences with systems of care. The perspectives and interests of families raising children with serious emotional disturbance governed all aspects of this study.

The family-driven study investigated the question, How does family engagement in systems of care affect child and family outcomes? The three goals (or purposes) of the study were to *(1)* study a question of interest to families in a manner that was rigorous and simultaneously consistent with the family values of systems of care; *(2)* support families to take the lead in all aspects of designing and conducting a study with highly qualified researchers playing a supportive role and providing technical assistance; and *(3)* document the experience, process, and lessons learned from making the paradigm shift (Osher & Osher, 2002) to doing research in this manner. So that other organizations, researchers, and family members in other communities could learn from this experience and develop their own capacity for meaningful research into topics of concern to them, members of the research study team consciously documented the challenges, opportunities, and lessons learned.

Instead of approaching the study with a set of predetermined study questions, the study team decided to be completely open and to engage families and individuals in the system of care and in the broader children's mental health community in identifying what should be studied. Using a modified Delphi process to generate and set priorities among a range of topics, the team established three research questions.

1. How are families engaged in systems of care?
2. What supports or inhibits family engagement in systems of care?
3. Is there a relationship between family engagement and child and family outcomes?

In the course of developing the research questions, it became apparent that there were many different perspectives on what constitutes family involvement. The team was most interested in purposeful activities as opposed to simply being present at a meeting or event. The team called this "engagement" and developed the following definition to insure a common understanding of the term: "Engagement is the act of doing something for your child, yourself, or your family that determines or derives from a care plan or supports the delivery of services and supports." Engagement can also be associated with participation of families and youth with the intention of improving or enhancing system planning and the overall delivery of treatment, services, family supports, or care. Other terms typically used to refer to these acts are "involvement," "participation," "advocating," "seeking," "facilitating," and "evaluating."

While field testing the study questions, the team also got family input on the best methods for gathering data to answer the questions. The result was a study design that used mixed-method—a self-administered mail survey, focus groups, and data from the longitudinal study of the national evaluation of the Comprehensive Community Mental Health for Children and Their Families Programs. This combined quantitative-qualitative approach provided richer results than one method alone could provide. Both the survey and the focus group protocol were approved by the Office of Management and Budget (OMB). Approval for the study was also obtained by the institutional review board (IRB) at ORC Macro, and the IRBs at the three systems-of-care communities that served as data collection sites.

Findings

The survey and focus group protocols gathered data about how families perceived their engagement in systems of care. This included finding what activities they engaged in, what made it easy or difficult to be engaged, and what perceived impact their engagement had on their child and family. Highlights of the findings are briefly summarized here.

Ways Families Are Engaged

Overall, activities that provided support to the family and direct involvement in their child's treatment were most common. The participants tended to be less engaged in activities that had an impact on the system of care or children's mental health policy. Being involved with activities conducted by a family-run organization, active participation in their child's treatment, and participation in team meetings for their child accounted for 48% of the responses, while only three individuals reported doing advocacy work and two reported being involved in their system of care evaluation.

What Supports Engagement?

Support services and information as well as opportunities for personal growth leading to empowerment and advocacy were the dominant themes among the 104 responses about what supports family involvement. Being respected by professionals for their intelligence and involvement, and having a better understanding of where to access information were representative responses. About one-third of the responses identified services, supports, and information as contributing to positive outcomes. Examples included having trust in the case manager or therapist and the knowledge to interact with school personnel.

Outcomes Families Attribute to Engagement

Families attributed positive outcomes to development of their own empowerment and their own participation in services. Increased and improved care and services accounted for more than half of the positive outcomes families perceived. Typical of the scenarios mentioned were examples of how being engaged facilitated getting services that prevented court involvement. Having mentors, family counseling, pre-crisis planning, family therapy, social activities, and recreation for siblings were the kinds of services families attributed to their engagement. Other positive changes identified were personal growth or self-awareness, including empowerment, and changes in their child's behavior or functioning. "We are more apt and quicker to tell a treatment provider, 'thanks, but no thanks,'" was a typical response.

Barriers to Engagement

Predominately families indicated that what inhibits their involvement were factors that limited their access to services. Specific issues mentioned were time constraints, lack of resources close to home, "revolving therapists," and waiting lists. A paucity of appropriate clinical services or support services (such as child care and transportation) and poor relationships with providers and systems, characterized by lack of trust, negative attitudes toward families, and stigma were frequently identified barriers. Inadequate or inaccurate information and poor communication were also mentioned.

Role of Researchers and Families

The project began late in 1999 with recruitment of a team to design and conduct the study. Regional and cultural diversity were taken into consideration in selecting members who were linked with active family organizations or youth groups and who had some experience and interest in research and evaluation. The original team was comprised of four family members (from Florida, Georgia, Maryland, and Utah), one youth (from Minnesota), and one senior researcher from ORC Macro International. During the course of the study, ORC Macro assigned a variety of staff to the team and the youth member left to pursue other interests and was replaced by another family member from the same background. One of the family members was designated as the principal investigator and one as the project director. Work was done by conference calls, e-mail, and an occasional face-to-face meeting. More than half of the team members had personal experience with federally funded system-of-care communities. All team members were fairly compensated for their time and expenses associated with doing this work.

The expectation has been that the family members on the team would be responsible for making decisions about all aspects of the work. In practice, leadership was truly a collaboration between the principal investigator, the project director, and the ORC Macro researcher. The challenge for the researcher/advisor was in suspending his or her own judgment and allowing the decision to be made by the team. The challenges for the family members were to keep asking questions to gain a full understanding before making each decision and resist the tendency to automatically defer to the expertise of the researcher/advisor.

The ORC Macro researcher role was to provide the rest of the team with information about the various options and their implications. For example, when preparing materials to get clearance from the Office of Budget and Management (OMB), the researcher provided the team with a chart detailing four different ways to identify families and get their consent to participate in the study. The team discussed the pros and cons of each option, including the financial and human cost, before making its final choice.

The ORC Macro staff assigned to the team provided technical expertise and guidance to support the decisions made by the family members on the team. They also provided or arranged for training for the team on topics and processes as needed. The training was both informal and formal in nature, but all of the assistance was provided when it was most needed in the course of the study. The specific content areas covered included the following:

- Basics of research
- Delphi process
- Determining study methodology
- Designing and implementing focus groups
- Developing logic models
- Questionnaire construction
- Development of focus group moderator guides
- Development of informed consent forms and confidentiality procedures
- Development of OMB and IRB protocols
- Data collection
- Data analysis and development of database for questionnaire data
- Analysis of focus group data
- Report writing

The ORC Macro staff and family members have jointly and individually written articles on the study (ORC Macro, 2001). The entire team has collaborated on PowerPoint presentations that various members have given at national conferences.

Family member and researcher roles were not formally prescribed at the outset of the study. Clarity about individual responsibilities has evolved over time. Fortunately, there was a sincere mutual respect among all team members from the very start. This has fostered trust and enabled the team to work smoothly without a hierarchical structure or hard and fast rules. In a less congenial setting it would be useful to be specific about roles and responsibilities from the outset.

Challenges

Keeping team members engaged during slower phases of the work (such as waiting for clearance from OMB) and on task required constant attention from the project director and the principal investigator. Scheduling conference calls and keeping in touch with team members in several states and different time zones was difficult. Family members, especially those who devote only a few hours per month to this activity, were easily distracted by more pressing work in their local organizations as well as attending to the needs of their children and other family matters. Having very specific tasks with deadlines did help. Frequent e-mail and phone reminders were essential.

The family-driven study team seriously underestimated the time and effort involved in obtaining clearance from OMB to begin data collection. Being a substudy of the larger national evaluation of the Comprehensive Community Mental Health Services for Children and Their Families program further complicated the process. On the other hand, preparing the necessary documents for OMB review forced the team to consider and resolve critical issues for completing the work in an ethical and rigorous manner. The researcher/advisor of the ORC Macro staff was an invaluable support and resource for this aspect of the work, which was totally unfamiliar to most of the family members.

The family-driven study team, which was very diverse in all respects (culturally, racially, economically, geographically, experientially, and educationally), successfully operated by consensus. The small size of the group, its congeniality, the open-mindedness of the team members, and their willingness to listen were the keys to compromise. The intensive working face-to-face meetings included times for social interaction that strengthened the bonds between team members as individuals and as a group.

The biggest challenge for the family members of the team was realizing that they could not "speak" as the sole voice for families in designing the study. They had taken on the role of researchers and, therefore, had to devise ways to keep checking with grassroots families to insure the "friendliness" of the questions and data collection process. For example, family team members conducted focus groups in their home communities to "test" the research questions under consideration and to learn which methods of data collection families preferred. This served to protect family members on the team from becoming so engrossed in the research process and requirements that they lost touch with a true family perspective.

Conclusions

The family-driven study team concluded that families of children enrolled in systems of care believe that their own engagement in those systems of care does have an impact on outcomes, whether this is supported by the formal clinical outcome data or not. Participating in treatment, being an active member of their child's treatment planning team, and participating in family-run organization activities appear to be the most frequently reported kinds of engagement families reported. Support services, positive relationships with peers and professionals, activities that enhance their knowledge and skills so they can be effective advocates for their child seem to be most valued by families. Functional (rather than clinical) outcomes also seem to be most valued by families. Outcomes that families value and attribute to their engagement with the system of care are not typically assessed by systems of care or the national evaluation. These include increased empowerment, improved care and services, increased family voice in advocacy, and greater levels of family support.

Participating in this study created an invaluable partnership between the family members of the study team and the ORC Macro staff. Family members became deeper thinkers around developing research questions and data analysis as a result of their participation in this study. Similarly, ORC Macro gained a better understanding for the context of the data. Team members represented various professional orientations, which made for interesting interpretations and creative solutions on how to further analyze the data. The partnership resulted in a shared learning process, which will continue as team members look toward identifying next steps.

Bonnie Bates (2005), the qualitative researcher who wrote a report documenting the history and lessons learned about doing family-driven research, concluded:

> Leaving research solely in the hands of researchers who have excellent research skills without a deep understanding of family issues leaves something out of the final picture. Family members can develop skills and knowledge to act as true partners in research and, further, to design and implement valid research studies with support from evaluators. The goal is for family members and researchers to create and conduct an ethical, meaningful, and useful product in partnership with one another.

YOUTH-DRIVEN RESEARCH PROJECT

The youth-driven research project was initiated to document and summarize the experiences of youth with co-occurring substance abuse and mental health disorders in a research process directed by the youth. The goals of the study were *(1)* to improve the understanding of the needs of youth with co-occurring mental health and substance abuse disorders and their families; and *(2)* to provide service providers and policy makers with better information on meeting the needs of these youth and their families. The study was conceived by the national Federation of Families for Children's Mental Health (FFCMH) in Alexandria, Virginia, and was funded by the Substance Abuse and Mental Health Services Administration (SAMHSA). FFCMH partnered with a state FFCMH chapter, Keys for Networking, Inc., in Topeka, Kansas, to implement the project. The National Federation of Families for Children's Mental Health and its affiliates have strongly advocated for the involvement of youth and families in the research process and saw the development of a nationwide youth-led project as an opportunity to demonstrate the viability of this model.

The project was grounded in two important premises: first, the youth would determine the focus of the research as well as carry out the study; second, the research would include youth voices from across the country and represent more than just one area or culture. Two lead youth researchers, Jill Schalansky and Rob Keeley, were identified and they contacted other youth who had co-occurring substance abuse and mental health disorders and invited them to participate in the project. They recruited youth from FFCMH board of directors, from FFCMH board's youth committee, and from statewide Federation of Families chapters, eventually developing a core group of 15 youth researchers. For over a year, this group connected with each other through weekly conference calls to identify the questions they wanted to answer, answers that would make their treatment better. Because of the distance, the planning had to be done by telephone. These youth, who had never met, spent the first several months sharing their experiences and developing a bond. All of the youth researchers had experienced residential treatment for both their mental health and substance use problems. Through sharing these experiences, the group built a foundation for collaboration.

The youth agreed to employ Melissa Nolte, PhD, an independent evaluator and qualitative researcher. As Jane Adams, executive director of Keys for Networking, Inc. and family member collaborator on the project, recalled, "Melissa didn't just one day come into a meeting and say 'Okay, I'm the researcher.' Melissa supported this study with her expertise. She agreed to refine the work of the youth and to work at their directions—to study what they wanted to learn." The youth researchers decided that conducting focus groups with youth and families across several states would be the most effective way to gather information. Youth researchers facilitated the focus groups and partnered with Federation-affiliated chapters to secure participants. Melissa Nolte trained the youth researchers to facilitate focus groups. Keys for Networking staff mailed each youth researcher a focus group "tool kit" that included such things as written guidelines for conducting the focus group, audiotapes and tape recorder, confidentiality statements, and postage. Several focus group practice sessions were conducted via telephone with Melissa as the instructor and consultant who was alert for potential problems.

Theme Development

Once the focus groups were completed, the youth researchers returned all information to the Keys for Networking office. The tapes were transcribed and the transcripts were taken apart in order to group the responses and comments on each question together. This initial analysis was sent to the youth researchers to verify that the responses fit with their experiences as facilitators. The youth were instrumental in deriving the final themes, making decisions about interpretation and serving as the touchstones for the analysis. "The research team felt very strongly about who was qualified to analyze the data. They did not want to have some 'outsider' or a person removed from the data analyze it" (Federation of Families for Children's Mental Health, 2001, p. 12). At first it was difficult to convince the youth that they had the authority to decide what the findings meant. Jane Adams recalls that it was a challenge "getting the kids to really believe that we meant it, that they could decide things." Once they accepted this, they spoke up when they felt the information was not being presented accurately. The youth were most excited about the interpretation of the data. As Jane Adams recalled, "Getting them to participate on planning calls and getting trained, that was hard. But involving them in the interpretation was easy. They were eager to inspect the collective experience of the focus groups and to relate their own individual experiences to the data."

To examine the themes more closely and to develop an interpretation of the themes, Keys for Networking and the national Federation staff convened the youth researchers, adult collaborators, and selected parents and youth who represented the diversity of the focus group participants at a conference in Kansas City. This diverse group came together for a "member check" regarding the analysis of the data, reviewed the themes, and developed recommendations. With such strong emotions associated with the subject matter, the conference was carefully planned to accommodate the need for building trust between participants and their need to express their anxieties and expectations.

Jill Schalansky, lead youth researcher, does not believe that a traditional researcher could have obtained the type of information that the youth researchers gathered. The youth researchers understood the importance of sharing their experiences with those youth who were participating in the focus groups. For every focus group question asked, the youth researchers answered it first themselves, sharing their experience of the mental health and substance abuse facilities and establishing a connection with the other participants. This helped the youth in the focus groups feel more comfortable sharing their information with the youth researchers and helped elicit honest and in-depth responses. As Jill recalled, "As we got deeper and the questions became harder, they were like—This person knows what's going on. They've been here and experienced it."

The Findings

The themes derived from the focus group data suggest that youth from seven states across the United States with co-occurring mental health and substance abuse disorders and their families rarely receive the type of help they need when they need it. They reported services that were fragmented, rigid, and unresponsive to the real needs of the youth. Both youth researchers and their adult collaborators were surprised by some of the findings. Youth and parents who participated in the focus groups reported that service providers never asked them what they thought about the services they received. Melissa Nolte was surprised that "it was alien to be asking youth what they think they've gone through." Similarly, Jill Schalansky noted that "None of the kids were asked how they liked their services after they were done...I asked that question and I think I had kids laugh at me."

An important component of the project for the youth researchers was to make recommendations about what things are helpful and what does work. They developed recommendations directed at a range of people, including providers, families, youth, and SAMHSA. Jane Adams, executive director of Keys for Networking commented, "The way this information was disseminated, I believe, was as important as what the information was." The research team of youth and adult collaborators decided to present the findings in a medium that speaks to youth and families: a play. Participants told their stories and in so doing educated the audience about what they had experienced, what they needed, and what must be changed in order to effectively serve youth with co-occurring substance abuse and mental health disorders and their families. Using this format, the youth researchers along with collaborating adults presented their findings to SAMHSA in October 2000 and at the FFCMH Annual Conference in November 2000.

Benefits and Challenges

The information gathered by these youth depicts the services and supports available for youth with co-occurring mental health and substance abuse disorders and the challenges they face. Over 150 people from different communities shared their stories with the youth researchers. Jane Adams said, "There is a real truth to it. It's not somebody opening a curtain and looking onto something. It really is what happened to these people." The involvement of youth with co-occurring mental health and substance abuse disorders as the researchers in this project played a direct role in the collection of these very powerful stories. Jane Adams noted that the information gathered had so much impact "because the people who experienced it said it was the truth and it had to be their questions, not questions I probably would have asked."

Because all of the collaborators understood the potential power that these youth researchers had in reporting their experiences, the challenges that emerged were resolved. One such challenge, as Melissa Nolte pointed out, was the length of time it took to complete the research. Conducting this research took much longer because it was a collaborative process and because all the planning as well as data analysis (except for the conference and presentations) was done by telephone. On reflection, Melissa recommended doing such a collaborative project in circumstances where youth researchers and their adult collaborators can have more face-to-face contact.

Another challenge was finding youth who were in the right place in their lives to participate in the research. For the most part this meant finding youth researchers who were far enough past their own treatment experiences to reflect upon it, but who had not yet moved on to other interests and adult pursuits. Once identified, all the youth researchers were invested in the research project. They all had a strong motivation to change the situations faced by other youth and a desire to improve services. Jill Schalansky recalled that it was not hard to keep the youth researchers involved: "Part of what kept everybody interested was their desire to change it (the treatment services), and their desire to change the status quo." However, as described by Jane Adams, there is a short time period for the youth researcher to be interested in working on a project like this. The youth researchers who participated in this project are now adults, have appropriately moved on to other things, and will not be able to participate in another study together as youth. It is unlikely that adult collaborators will be able to work with the same group of youth researchers over time. Therefore, mechanisms for periodically recruiting, orienting, and training youth to the research process need to be built into plans for ongoing youth involvement in research. The youth researchers involved in this study are a valuable resource and, as adults, can serve as mentors to other youth researchers. In addition, involvement in a project like this can help to educate youth about the power of research and may potentially encourage youth to develop additional research skills (e.g., one youth researcher who worked on this project is currently working toward her PhD).

Neither the youth researchers nor their adult collaborators realized the impact their research findings would have or the interest it would generate. A written report, *Blamed and ashamed: The treatment experiences of youth with co-occuring substance abuse and mental health disorders and their families* (Federation of Families for Children's Mental Health, 2001), was printed and SAMSHA has published the report on their website. Staff at SAMSHA also funded a printing of 5000 copies of the report in 2001 and has made a commitment to a second printing. The findings were also referenced in the 2002 Report to Congress on the Prevention and Treatment of Co-occuring Substance Abuse Disorders and Mental Disorders. Bert Pepper, MD, who has done research on co-occurring mental health and substance abuse disorders over the past 20 years, reviewed the report and commented on the significance of the findings. The youth researchers invited Dr. Pepper to present with them at the FFCMH annual conference in 2000, where he remarked on how similar the findings were to the findings in some of his studies.

The youth-driven research project required substantial resources in the form of money, time, and contributions from the many adult collaborators. Both the Federation of Families for Children's Mental Health and their Kansas affiliate, Keys for Networking, made significant contributions by allowing their organizational infrastructure and fundraising skills to support the youth researchers and the research activities. This project demonstrates, however, that youth who have experienced the mental health and substance abuse services system have the capacity, the commitment, and the knowledge to contribute significantly to the research process and provide leadership and direction to the research enterprise. Without the involvement of the youth researchers a different story would have been told from a different perspective, probably in less depth and with less meaningful results.

EVALUATOR PERSPECTIVES ON COLLABORATION WITH FAMILY MEMBERS

Researchers at the RTC are engaged in an ongoing study of the perspectives of individuals employed as evaluators in system-of-care sites funded through the Comprehensive Community Mental Health Services for Children and their Families Program. The grant funding recommends that family members be fully involved as team members in the evaluation process, and evaluators at these grant communities around the country are now working in partnership with family members.

Based on a review of literature and a series of informal conversations with evaluators, a qualitative research study was developed to examine the experiences of evaluators working with family members on evaluation teams. Open-ended questions were designed to identify the roles that family members play on evaluation teams, evaluators' preparation for this work in their training, barriers to family involvement in evaluation, and effective strategies for collaborating with family members.

Evaluators were identified through processes of expert nomination and snowball sampling. To date, 18 evaluators have participated in semi-structured telephone or face-to-face interviews, and the following discussion is based on theme analysis of the information they provided (Morse, 1994). The participants were 14 females and 4 males and all were Caucasian. Thirteen evaluators had obtained PhD degrees, two were engaged in doctoral studies, two had Masters degrees, and one had two Bachelors degrees. The mean age of participants was 41.8 years (range 28–66 years), and they had worked in the field of children's mental health for an average of 13.5 years (range 3–30 years). All respondents reported being unprepared by their training to work in partnership with family members in evaluation, and they described varying degrees of openness to collaboration. Twelve of the 18 evaluators reported that they or someone in their family had experience as a consumer of mental health services.

Detailed verbatim notes were made during the interviews and these notes were examined in the light of the five core principles identified by McKay (Chapter Two, this volume) as impacting the process and outcome of collaboration. While not explicitly guiding the design of this research, which was developed to examine evaluator constructions of collaborative evaluation in an emergent way (Rodwell, 1998), these principles were used as a framework for examining the interview findings, as described below.

Agreement and Investment in Shared Goals

According to these evaluators, shared goals did not emerge easily. Researchers and family members are likely to share the goal to improve services for children with serious emotional disorders and their families. Researchers and evaluators are inclined to take a long-term perspective, seeing the change process occurring through rigorous research design and systematic data gathering procedures, while family members, impatient for rapid change, may embrace advocacy as a strategy for change. One evaluator referred to her "fear that parents might take the data and interpret and use the results beyond how they should be used."

The tension between concern for rigorous research and evaluation and the desire for immediate change was described as leading to stress and even some conflict between evaluators and family members. Examples of teams' inability to negotiate conflicting goals were described, and in a few instances the family member decided she was unsuited for this work and quit the job. An evaluator reported that a family member "became frustrated and left because she could see problems and couldn't see how to fix them... at heart, she was an advocate and wanted to make changes." In retrospect, the evaluator acknowledged that she had learned a lot from this experience: "I didn't anticipate and help her deal with the stress."

In other cases, team members were able to negotiate complementary goals or subsidiary goals, so that the work could proceed. One evaluator talked about introducing logic modeling to the team as a strategy for eliciting and sharing ideas about goals and tying the evaluation to agreed upon goals. Others reported that they spent considerable time discussing and reconciling goals.

Equitable Distribution of Power, Including Fair Involvement in Decision Making and Opportunities to Influence Interpretation of Study Findingss

The evaluation projects described in this study did not exemplify equitable distribution of power because the professionally trained evaluators were employed as principal investigators. These principal researchers were responsible for ensuring that the work was completed in a timely manner, which included hiring, supervising, and training family members to do the work. On the other hand, there were numerous reports of sharing power within team processes. Evaluators described their efforts to work in partnership with family evaluators, who had influence in decision making regarding the design of questions and instruments, data collection, analysis, and reporting of findings.

Family members were described as having specific influence in the data analysis stage, which shifted evaluators' perspectives on objectivity in the research process. Several participants described incidents where family members had questioned or challenged their preliminary interpretations of data and upon further analysis, the team discovered that there had been an error or misinterpretation. One evaluator said,

> I've had situations where [family member] saved us on some pretty big stuff. Just by saying, "You know I don't think that data's right"... and you know either we had re-coded wrong or in one case once we had gotten more data and the thing just washed out... I've learned not to just say, "Oh, you've got to look at the data because the data's right."

Recognition of Skills and Expertise Associated with Both University Training and Community Experience

Evaluators offered a range of perspectives on family member skills and expertise and their own skills. One evaluator emphasized the unique strengths of all team members: a parent who was good with numbers was asked to help with data analysis, while one with strong advocacy skills was asked to present findings. Special talents and skills of specific family members were reported as eliciting the respect of team members. For example, an evaluator described a family evaluator as having "personality characteristics that make you a good researcher, regardless of family status, for example, she is very detail-oriented. She has innate characteristics that lend themselves to the job—thoughtful, curious."

Barriers related to this principle were addressed in two domains of concern: respect for the skills and expertise of all team members; and recognition for family members' expertise in terms of adequate compensation. Evaluators' initial attitudes toward family members appeared to be related to training. All participants reported that their university training had not prepared them to collaborate with families and some were initially hesitant. One evaluator who was trained to value technical expertise admitted thinking at first that it was "ridiculous" to hire family members to work in evaluation. Over time he has changed his perspective on objectivity and learned to appreciate the knowledge that family members bring to the collaboration. In some cases, family members "earned" respect by demonstrating capacity to be effective participants in the research.

One evaluator reported that when she finished school, she had technical skills but she was "not trained to communicate in the real world." She said that she preferred collaborative research with family members because her previous research "wasn't making a difference in the real world." Within teams, evaluators promoted respect for family members' expertise and capacity for objectivity, with some success, but they also faced challenges among service providers, exemplified by this comment: "Over time they are gaining respect as they work with [family members] more. The main issue is perception regarding objectivity." Some evaluators also reported a parallel struggle to overcome biases against them specifically and evaluation generally. A participant reported dealing with "the perception that evaluation is complicated, boring, and useless among families and service providers." According to one evaluator, gaining recognition of her skills involved mutual learning, asking questions, and listening well, a process as having to "de-bunk the myths" about evaluation.

Recognition of family members' skills was also sought through adequate salaries. The lack of reasonable compensation for family evaluators was described as a challenge at the institutional level. Participants in teams under the auspices of universities reported that salary levels were fixed according to educational qualifications. There were serious salary differentials between professionally trained evaluators and family evaluators without a college degree. Despite low salaries, some family members lost their eligibility for public mental health services because their salary placed them above the income limit for their state's Medicaid program. Family members on low incomes were also disadvantaged by slow reimbursement for research expenses.

Ongoing Opportunities for Communication Based upon Commitment to Honest Exchanges and Willingness to Raise Concerns without Blame

Participants described strategies to increase open communication, such as asking for family members' input, listening carefully, treating all team members with respect, and sharing the frustrations of doing the work together. Being "up-front," speaking up, and not being afraid to be a professional were mentioned as contributing to a culture of openness and honesty. Evaluators took responsibility for "demystifying the research process" and "reducing the intimidation factor" as ways to increase the confidence of family members. There were efforts to promote a culture of learning by doing, with evaluators expressing their openness to learning from the family members. A recurring theme in evaluators' comments was their willingness to try new approaches, to experiment with new strategies, to "think outside the box," and to be willing to make mistakes and learn from them. There was emphasis on building a team as a learning community "that values everyone's opinions."

While family evaluators were hired for their knowledge and skills as family members who had negotiated the service delivery system, few of them had research skills when they began the work. As the evaluation project proceeded, there was a growing realization of the need for technical skills in data entry and analysis, report writing, and presentation of findings. Evaluators assisted family members to identify their needs for training for the technical aspects of the research. In some instances they reported providing on-site training or encouraging family members to attend the Federation of Families training, and/or training at local community colleges and universities.

Trust

Trust was described as a vital element of effective collaboration. One evaluator acknowledged the question of trust from the family perspective: "Am I coming in to use them or help them in some way?" With this question in mind, she structured the team's activities to demonstrate her appreciation for family members' knowledge and flexibility to accommodate their need to find a balance between family responsibilities and getting the work done. Other recommended strategies for building trust included "being open to learning in a bidirectional manner" and asking questions such as, "What outcomes do you think are important to look for?"

Developing nurturing relationships to manage the stress of the job was described as a key element of building trust. One evaluator attributed her team's trusting relationships to their emphasis on getting "to know each other as people" and having a "family-friendly environment." She said that the trust was perceived through a flexible work environment with a "culture of working 40 hours," but "not specific hours... Just do what needs to be done." To accommodate family evaluators' schedule challenges associated with frequent crises resulting from their child's condition, flexibility was needed. If anyone fell behind with his or her work, this team had evolved a system whereby others would help that person.

Trust was reported as easier to develop by evaluators who were seen as having an investment in the community. Two evaluators reported that they had returned to the rural community that had been their childhood home and that this enhanced their credibility in the community. Several participants reported that they had been trained as social workers and this training had prepared them well for developing trusting relationships with others.

This review of qualitative responses suggests that McKay's principles were considered as goals by these evaluators. While these evaluators addressed the topic areas of the principles, they referred to them as ideals rather than achieved states. They described many barriers and challenges to achieving ideal forms of the principles. It appears that these evaluators were committed to working collaboratively with family members because they perceived the benefits of family involvement, such as more relevant research, better response rates, more detailed and possibly more honest answers from evaluation respondents, and more accurate interpretation of data. With these benefits in mind, these evaluators described their investment in struggling to overcome the challenges to collaborative evaluation.

CONCLUSIONS AND DISCUSSION

The examples described in this chapter allow the reader to experience in detail both the benefits and challenges of youth and family collaboration with academic researchers. Each of the sections reported that collaboration between family, youth, and academic researchers resulted in a better research product; research that asked questions thought to be more relevant to the needs and preferences of families and youth, data sets that were more complete, with more detail and in-depth responses, and findings that had been more thoroughly assessed in the face of reality and the practical experience of the consumer. A number of challenges also emerge from the examples provided here. The time and investment of resources required to develop a collaborative relationship was emphasized in all of the sections. Not only did it take time for the academic researchers to earn the trust of the families and youth, but it also took time for the group of family members (as in the family-driven research study) and the group of youth (in the youth-driven research project) to develop relationships within their groups, to come to agreement about the goals of their projects, and to figure out how decisions would be made among them. As McKay (Chapter Two, this volume) notes, skills and expertise developed in ways other than academic training need to be recognized to make the research collaboration productive. In our examples, the family researchers working with the Clark County evaluation found their skills questioned by some commu-nity members, who wondered if the family members could objectively collect data about services their child may have received. This did not seem to be an issue for the family-driven or youth-driven projects. In these two projects, the very act of placing the families and youth in the lead researcher position delivered a clear message about the values of their knowledge and experience.

In our view there are two major challenges to future research collaborations between family members, youth, and academic researchers. The first is the challenge associated with influencing policy makers and funding mechanisms to seek out and fully fund family- and youth-driven studies. Both projects reported on here were funded by the SAMHSA and signal a strong commitment to family and youth involvement in the development of services and to understanding what it means to experience those services. All those in the position to fund research and evaluation need to be encouraged to take similar action, making sure that their research priorities, review processes, and funding procedures allow family and youth researchers to serve as principal investigators or co-researchers.

A second challenge emerges from the variety of federally mandated evaluations, many that currently require or strongly encourage the involvement of consumers and/or family members in evaluations that are directed by academic researchers.

This kind of pressure from funders is useful in getting more families and youth involved, but in order for this approach to produce useful new knowledge, additional supports and new methods needs to be developed. Researchers need a different kind of training and an opportunity to learn from each other and from their collaborators in order to approach the partnership in a way that is likely to build trust and result in a useful research. Just as family members are developing skills as researchers and evaluators, researchers are being called on to develop skills in communication and ways of sharing power. From the examples described in this chapter, it is clear that the benefits derived from the research collaboration are well worth the adaptations that may need to be made by individuals.

Acknowledgments. Preparation of this chapter was supported in part by the Research and Training Center on Family Support and Children's Mental Health, Regional Research Institute for Human Services, Portland State University, grant H133B990025, National Institute on Disability and Rehabilitation Research, U.S. Department of Education, and Center for Mental Health Services, Substance Abuse and Mental Health Services Administration. The views expressed in this chapter are not necessarily those of the funders.

References

Allen, D. A., & Stefanowski-Hudd, S. (1987). Are we professionalizing parents? Weighing the benefits and pitfalls. *Mental Retardation, 25*(3), 133–139.

Arnstein, S. R. (1969). A ladder of citizen participation. *AIP Journal, 35*(4), 216–224.

Bates, B. (2005). *The family-driven research study: Lessons learned by families and researchers working together.* Atlanta, GA: ORC Macro.

Checkoway, B. (1979). Citizens on local health planning boards: What are the obstacles? *Journal of Community Development Society, 10*(2), 101–116.

Chu, F. D., & Trotter, S. (1974). *The madness establishment: Ralph Nader's Study Group Report on the National Institute of Mental Health.* Oxford, England: Grossman.

Comprehensive Community Mental Health Services for Children with Serious Emotional Disturbances Act. (1992). Public law 102-321, as amended Part E, Title V, Sections 561–565.

DeJong, G. (1979). Independent living: From social movement to analytic paradigm. *Archives of Physical Medicine and Rehabilitation, 60,* 435–446.

Elliott, D., Koroloff, N., Koren, P. E., & Friesen, B. J. (1998). *Improving access to children's mental health services: The family associates approach.* Austin, TX: Pro-ed.

Federation of Families for Children's Mental Health. (2001). *Blamed and ashamed: The treatment experience of youth with co-occurring substance abuse and mental health disorders and their families.* Alexandria, VA: Federation of Families for Children's Mental Health.

Federation of Families for Children's Mental Health. (2002). *The world of evaluation: How to make it yours.* Unpublished training materials. www.ffcmh.org

Hall, B. (1993). Introduction. In P. Park, M. Brydon-Miller, B. Hall, & T. Jackson (Eds.), *Voices of change: Participatory research in the United States and Canada* (pp. xiv–xii). Westport, CT: Bergen and Garvey.

Koroloff, N., & Friesen, B. (1997). Challenges in conducting family-centered mental health services research. *Journal of Emotional and Behavioral Disorders, 5*(3), 130–137.

Koroloff, N., Friesen, B., Reilly, L., & Rinkin, J. (1996). The role of family members in systems of care. In B. Stroul (Ed.), *Children's mental health: Creating systems of care in a changing society* (pp. 409–426). Baltimore: Paul H. Brookes.

Koseki, L. K. (1977). Consumer participation in health maintenance organizations. *Health and Social Work, 2*(4), 51–69.

Maclure, R. (1990). The challenge of participatory research and its implications for funding agencies. *International Journal of Sociology and Social Policy, 10*(3), 1–21.

Morse, J. M. (1994). "Emerging from the data": The cognitive processes of analysis in qualitative inquiry. In J. M. Morse (Ed.)., *Critical issues in qualitative research methods* (pp. 23–43). Thousand Oaks, CA: Sage Publications.

Nancarrow, C., & Brace, I. (2000). Saying the "right thing": Coping with social desirability bias in marketing research. *Bristol Business School Teaching and Research Review, 3*, 1–12.

ORC Macro, Int. (2001). The family-driven research study. *System of Care Evaluation Briefs, 3*(1), 1–4.

Osher, T., & Osher, D. (2002). The paradigm shift to true collaboration with families, *The Journal of Child and Family Studies, 11*(1), 47–60.

Osher, T., Van Kammen, W., & Zaro, S. (2001). Family participation in evaluating systems of care: Family, research and services system perspectives. *Journal of Emotional and Behavioral Disorders, 9*(1), 63–70.

Pinto R., & Fiester, A. (1979). Governing board and management staff attitudes toward community mental health center citizen participation. *Community Mental Health Journal, 15*(4), 259–266.

Rodwell, M. K. (1998). *Social work constructivist research.* New York: Garland Publishing, Inc.

Rogers, E. S., & Palmer-Erbs, V. (1994). Participatory action research: Implications for research and evaluation in psychiatric rehabilitation. *Psychosocial Rehabilitation Journal, 18*(2), 3–12.

Santelli, B., Ginsberg, C., Sullivan, S., & Niederhauser, C. (2002). A collaborative study of parent to parent programs: Implications for positive behavior support. In J. M. Lucyshyn, G. Dunlap, & R. W. Albin (Eds.), *Families and positive behavior support: Addressing problem behavior in family contexts* (pp. 439–456). Baltimore: Paul H. Brookes.

Shaughnessy, J. J., & Zechmeister, E. B. (1990). *Research methods in psychology* (3rd edition). New York: McGraw-Hill.

Stroul, B. A., & Friedman, R. M. (1986). *A system of care for severely emotionally disturbed children and youth.* Washington, DC: CASSP Technical Assistance Center.

Turnbull, A. P., Friesen, B. J., & Ramirez, C. (1998). Participatory action research as a model for conducting family research. *Journal for the Association for Persons with Severe Handicaps, 23*(3), 178–188.

Windle, C., & Cibulka, J. G. (1981). A framework for understanding participation in community mental health services. *Community Mental Health Journal, 17*(1), 4–18.

Chapter Four

Perspectives of Community Providers on Research Partnerships

Robert Abramovitz and Mimi Abramovitz

It seems logical that practitioners and researchers should work together to examine the delivery of mental health and social services because this might lead to improved quality of care for clients. Nonetheless, the historical record contains more examples of failure than success. Long-standing differences in the mission and methods of each partner have traditionally complicated the effort, leading to resistance by practitioners and frustration among researchers (U.S. Public Health Service Office of the Surgeon General, 1999). However, the advent of new regulatory mandates to achieve wide dissemination of evidence-based treatments has increasingly pressed practitioners and researchers to overcome these barriers and to find ways to work together to close the "critical gaps between optimally effective treatment and what many individuals receive in actual practice settings" (U.S. Public Health Service Office of the Surgeon General, 1999). The National Institute of Mental Health (NIMH) has concluded that the formation of such partnerships—defined as a relationship between individuals or groups characterized by mutual cooperation and responsibility for the achievement of a specified goal—can effectively promote real-world effectiveness studies and more rapid adoption of evidence-based treatment (National Advisory Mental Health Council, 1999).

This chapter advances the development of successful partnerships between practitioners and researchers by *(1)* identifying the need for the two-way exchange of knowledge between practice and research, *(2)* highlighting the value of researcher–practitioner partnerships, *(3)* presenting an illustrative case study of one agency's successful work in this area, and *(4)* making recommendations for change.

THE IMPORTANCE OF THE EXCHANGE AND DIFFUSION OF KNOWLEDGE BETWEEN RESEARCHERS AND PRACTITIONERS

The Institute of Medicine recently reported that "it takes an average of 17 years for research-generated knowledge to be incorporated into practice" (Institute of

Medicine, 2001). The acute need to "bridge the gap" more quickly has increased interest in determining the best ways to diffuse new knowledge from one arena to the other; to disseminate, adopt, and adapt new treatment approaches; and to define and overcome any obstacles to their use with fidelity and flexibility.

According to Weisz, Donenberg, Susan, and Weiss (1995), "The benefits of lab–clinic collaboration seem likely to flow in both directions . . . application of research therapy principles and findings may help to enhance the effects of clinical practice . . ..Conversely, attempts to bring some of the more pristine laboratory procedures into clinics may prompt significant adjustments in those procedures." In the process, they add, it should be possible to identify changes needed to make lab-tested therapies effective in clinical practice. "Clinical researchers may have a great deal to learn from practicing clinicians, just as clinicians may learn useful new approaches from the research community. If the obstacles to researcher–clinician collaboration can be overcome, both groups may profit, and to the ultimate benefit of the children and families who seek help" (Weisz et al., 1995). Furthermore, finding ways to improve the translation of research findings into routine clinical practice can meld the professional expectations of both mental health practitioners and researchers in the service of improving the quality of care for children.

THE FORMATION OF PARTNERSHIPS

In its report *Bridging Science and Service*, the NIMH identified "working partnerships between academic researchers and frontline service providers as the crux of efforts to develop the types of research. . .needed to improve the quality of care and the public health impact of the research." The report also identified the components of a successful alliance. They include *(a)* selecting topics of mutual concern; *(b)* ensuring benefits to all parties; *(c)* requiring that participants contribute a needed role or service; *(d)* designing studies with time frames appropriate to each partner; *(e)* maintaining contiguity of relationships to promote ongoing access and follow-through; *(f)* nurturing good relationships at all levels of the partnership; and *(g)* using partner's time efficiently (National Advisory Mental Health Council, 1999).

BRIDGING THE GAP: FROM THE PERSPECTIVE OF A COMMUNITY-BASED AGENCY

A recent exhaustive literature review found only limited models that demonstrate how to create partnerships at the agency level (Reback, Cohen, Freese, & Shoptaw, 2002) and few if any reports evaluating the impact of such partnerships on the community-based partner (Currie et al., 2005). The following case study written from the perspective of a community-based agency—the Jewish Board of Family and Children's Services (JBFCS) in New York City—adds to the literature by discussing the various efforts the agency made during the past 30 years to integrate practice and research. The case study *(a)* illustrates the rationale, importance, and benefits of its various approaches; *(b)* identifies success principles; *(c)* describes obstacles to collaboration; and *(d)* makes recommendations for improvements.

The Setting

The Jewish Board of Family and Children's Services (JBFCS) is not a typical freestanding community-based program. One of New York City's oldest and largest mental health and social service agencies, JBFCS operates more than 170 community-based programs at sites throughout New York City and Westchester County. This network of services includes 12 outpatient clinics, four residential treatment centers for children, three adolescent day treatment centers, and two adult day treatment centers, all of which on any particular day serve an average of 10,800 people of all religious, racial, ethnic, and socioeconomic backgrounds throughout the New York metropolitan area. Social workers comprise the majority of the primary service providers.

The Jewish Board of Family and Child Services resulted from the 1978 merger of two outstanding New York City–based social service and mental health agencies: Jewish Family Service (JFS) and Jewish Board of Guardians (JBG). Founded in 1874, JFS (a family mental health and social services agency) provided concrete relief to needy Jewish families and in the years following World War II pioneered the use of family therapy to treat emotional and personal problems. Founded in 1893 to rehabilitate child and adult delinquents, JBG (a child guidance agency) evolved into a national leader in the care of disturbed children using sophisticated psychiatric treatments. In the 1960s both agencies responded to the pervasive nature of problems plaguing families and children by expanding services to New Yorkers from all backgrounds. Meeting the needs of New York City's highly urbanized racially, ethnically, and culturally diverse population still defines the major clinical focus of JBFCS.

Prior to their merger the leadership of each agency placed a high value on making intellectual contributions to the field. In the years immediately following World War II each agency began to pioneer the use of new treatment approaches, such as family therapy and psychoanalytically oriented intensive individual treatment. Senior staff at each agency also regularly engaged in professional publication and conference presentation. JBFCS currently sustains the historic commitment of both agencies to the continuing education of their staff through an endowed Educational Institute. Advocacy and service innovation has also contributed to JBFCS's ongoing recognition as a leader within the service agency community.

The organizational culture of the JBFCS has also consistently supported research. Over the past 40 years the agency used three broad organizational models to integrate research into the overall agency culture: *(1)* the establishment of an independent internal department; *(2)* support for project-by-project external collaborations; and *(3)* the development of ongoing partnerships designed to create a positive proactive research climate throughout the agency. The following case examples illustrate each of these organizational models.

Agency Structure to Support Research

Prior to the merger of JFS and JBG, each agency engaged in mental health research. In 1948, JFS established a research department that used scientific methods to gain insight into the causes and treatment of family conflict. JBG also conducted numerous research studies on issues of residential care. In 1953, William Goldfarb, MD, began a study of childhood schizophrenia at the newly opened JBG Henry Ittleson Center for Child Research. This was the first time the agency used specific selection criteria and random assignment to either residential or day treatment. In 1962 an 8-month sociological observational study of the social system of delinquent adolescent boys at JBG's Hawthorne Center was completed (Polsky, 1962).

In 1967, JBG made research an essential aspect of work throughout the agency by establishing a formal Research and Development Center (RDC) within the agency designed to build on studies work started in the 50s and early 60s. That same year, the RDC produced a research instrument that measured psychological changes in children in treatment as part of an evaluative study begun in 1957. During this decade it also completed a 10-year National Institute of Mental Health–funded study of the role of child care workers in residential treatment.

This internal research structure was very productive, but it was not sustainable as a result of several limitations in its original design: *(1)* the research was highly individualized and was confined to a specific project spearheaded by a particular clinical investigator who was linked either to a specific program or to a project led by an academic researcher from outside the agency; *(2)* it did not create a "research-friendly" culture within the wider agency; *(3)* the project findings did not lead to practice changes; and *(4)* finally, there were no funds to build a research infrastructure independent of a specific project. Eventually, dwindling funds and the lack of integration of research and practice into the work at JBG led the agency to close the center in the early 80s.

External Collaboration

Between 1983 and 1988, following the close of the research center, JBFCS staff continued to conduct research studies. Lacking an internal research infrastructure, individual staff members interested in research developed ad hoc external collaborations with individual academic researchers to address a particular issue of mutual interest. For example, the NYC Administration for Children's Services funded a collaboration between the staff of the JBFCS Institute for Infants,

Children, and Families with the Columbia University School of Public Health to study the effectiveness of an onsite, small-group, peer-play intervention with 3- to 5-year-old children whose behavioral disruptiveness placed them at risk for a poor transition to kindergarten. Likewise frontline staff, MSW students, and senior staff seeking doctoral degrees pursued self-initiated, small-scale studies with the assistance of intermittent expert consultation. They examined issues, such as cult involvement, doubled-up families, remarriage and blended families, and the cultural competence of social work students. While successful, this project-by-project model was not designed to integrate research into agency practice. Nor did it yield any lasting research infrastructure

Ongoing Academic Partnership to Create a Proactive Research Climate

The ongoing gap between practice and research eventually led JBFCS to pursue still another model—one based on institutionalized partnership with universities and grounded in new organizational structures. Three such partnerships were initiated: *(1)* a long-standing partnership with Columbia University School of Social Work created to do research about social work practice; *(2)* a more recent partnership formed with academic medical centers that are part of the federally sponsored National Child Traumatic Stress Network (NCTSN), created to disseminate evidence-based trauma treatment models; and *(3)* a collaboration with the Division of Child and Adolescent Psychiatry at Mount Sinai School of Medicine, focused on creating an ongoing agency-based research infrastructure for studies on child trauma.

The Partnership between the Jewish Board of Family and Child Services and Columbia University School of Social Work

The unique partnership between JBFCS and the Columbia University School of Social Work (CUSSW) was institutionalized through the formation of the Center for the Study of Social Work Practice (CSSWP). Founded in 1988, the CSSWP was established to couple social work research more tightly with social work practice. Dr. Shirley Jenkins, a professor at Columbia University School of Social Work, was the driving force behind the creation of the CSSWP and its first director. She articulated its primary mission as the production of research findings that had utility for practice. She stated: "Elegance of design, sophistication of statistics, and soundness of theory are all beside the point if the problem which is addressed has little relevance to client needs or service delivery" (Jenkins, 1989).

The CSSWP created a formal infrastructure that since its inception has stimulated a great deal of collaborative research between the agency and the university. This includes participation in the large-scale Odyssey Project designed to address the pressing need for a more comprehensive empirical knowledge base about children entering out-of-home care and the services they receive (Guterman & Cameron, 1997). To this end, the Child Welfare League of America enlisted two dozen residential treatment and group home facilities to participate in a multiyear national longitudinal study of the psychosocial characteristics and outcomes of children served in child welfare. The CSSWP was the infrastructure that enabled this project. JBFCS clinical staff, led by a CUSSW faculty member and graduate student, contributed 3 years of data to the national database and generated published finding of their own. Another large-scale project—a multiyear NIMH-funded study—examined the impact of the introduction of the C-DISC, a standardized, computerized assessment procedure for children, into the intake process at several JBFCS community-based outpatient mental health clinics. For this study, the CSSWP collaborated with the New York State Psychiatric Institute and the Child and Adolescent Psychiatry Division of the Columbia University School of Medicine to determine whether this proven epidemiological tool would be of value in clinical practice. That is, would the tool improve clinical assessment, add to its efficiency, affect treatment, and be viewed as useful by clinicians and clients (Mullen, 1998)?

A third project of CSSWP was the 3-year intervention development study funded by NIMH to examine the implementation and impact of the Sanctuary model introduced into JBFCS residential treatment centers. Designed in collaboration with the newly formed JBFCS Center for Trauma Program Innovation (CTPI) (see below), the study examined the implementation and proximal effects of an intervention designed to reduce trauma-related symptoms of youth that place them at high risk for violent behavior, poor adjustment, and serious mental health difficulties (Rivard et al., 2003). The CSSWP also supports small studies by individual CUSSW faculty and/or JBFCS practitioners (e.g., the effectiveness of a time-limited group therapy for recently divorced parents).

The CSSWP model has numerous strengths. These include a formal contractual relationship between the two founding organizations; an endowment fund that supports center staff and activities; and a joint advisory committee that reviews all proposed projects to assure that they are consistent with the center's overall mission of promoting practice research across a broad range of topics. The model facilitates matches between social work faculty and JBFCS staff when their research interests dovetail. It helps faculty with preexisting research interests to find suitable program settings and populations for study and provides JBFCS research-oriented staff with expert consultation on research design. To date, this JBFCS/CUSSW collaboration has conducted more than 25 studies both large and small, held three national conferences, and published two books.

The challenges of the CSSWP partnership include finding a balance between the career interests and research agenda of junior faculty and the research needs of JBFCS staff. Another challenge is the time required for clinical researchers at JBFCS to develop proposals for their own research project or to find partners among Columbia faculty with research interests that mesh with the agency clinician. These realities have limited the ability of the CSSWP to reach beyond the senior levels of agency staff and administrators.

Two other types of university collaborations grew out of the work of the JBFCS Center for Trauma Program Innovation (CTPI). The CTPI was founded in 1998 to respond to the high prevalence of trauma exposure among the client population served in all JBFCS divisions. The CTPI fosters the introduction of trauma-informed knowledge and services into mental health and social service agencies through capacity building, promotes outcomes evaluation as a necessary part of any CTPI program implementation activity, and spearheads organizational change within JBFCS and other mental health and social service agencies. The presence of CTPI and its specialized focus provided a platform for creating long-term research/practice partnerships with major academic organizations.

From 1998 to 2001 CTPI developed its trauma-informed programs in various JBFCS divisions, trained staff, worked with community groups, and otherwise helped to establish the trauma paradigm as the agency's unifying conceptual framework. This included the above-noted Sanctuary research project. In 2002 CTPI partnered with the Mount Sinai School of Medicine's (MSSM) Child and Adolescent Psychiatry Division to conduct field-effectiveness studies and to develop a model for fostering a lasting research "culture" and infrastructure within JBFCS. Funded by the NIMH Research Infrastructure Support Program (RISP), this partnership, concentrated on two overarching research interests shared by both organizations: child trauma services and evidence-based treatment dissemination. With RISP funding and access to JBFCS outpatient clinics, a CTPI/Mt. Sinai team designed and implemented a study to ascertain how to best identify trauma disorders in children. The research is systematically comparing semi-structured trauma assessment to existing assessment procedures. It will also introduce and study the use of evidence-based trauma treatment into standard clinic treatment.

The preexisting relationship between CTPI and Mt Sinai enabled the partners to rapidly and successfully respond to the 9/11 crisis by mounting two significant post-9/11 interventions that combined services and research. In the first intervention, the CTPI–Mt Sinai team was selected by Child and Adolescent Treatment Services (CATS) Consortium to be one of its nine community agency-academic medical center partners. CATS operated on two fronts. It provided evidence-based treatment to youth affected by 9/11 and conducted a large-scale treatment replication study of the treatments used. The JBFCS/MSSM CATS partnership clinical treatment/research team provided services within each of the partner's existing service systems, that is, JBFCS's satellite clinics at Ground Zero high schools and the MSSM hospital outpatient clinic. The second CTPI/MSSM project—The Infant, Toddler, and Preschool 9/11 Program—had its own site and special clinical staff who screened, assessed, and provided dyadic treatment to families with children age 5 and under on 9/11 who were living adjacent to Ground Zero. This project provided a unique opportunity to study assessment and treatment methods for very young disaster/terrorism affected children.

The strength of the RISP includes it capacity to fund both partners that in turn allowed each to dedicate staff to work on collaborative research and infrastructure building. With the RISP, JBFCS has been helped to build the capacity of the agency to achieve several "vital" interests, including the desire to routinely evaluate the effectiveness of its practice and to promote the adoption and dissemination of evidence-based practice. Maintaining a trauma-only focus carries the risk of too narrowly confining a critical mass of assets and research activity. However, because so many JBFCS clients have been exposed to traumatic events, this has not been a limiting factor. These agency–university partnerships inform agency practice by using state-of-the-art approaches to evaluate the effectiveness of standard practice, to adopt efficacious treatments, to field test the effectiveness of these treatments in a real-world context, and to enhance their external validity by informing researchers about clinician and client realities.

The existence of the CTPI also provided the platform for it to become a community treatment services partner within the National Child Traumatic Stress Network (NCSTN). This national organization's purpose is to identify, develop, and disseminate state-of-the-art evidence-based treatment models to improve the quality of treatment for traumatized children. Funded by the Substance Abuse and Mental Health Administration (SAMHSA), NCTSN membership has allowed CTPI to provide leadership in trauma-focused service development and to engage in other studies of the effectiveness of evidence-based practice by forming partnerships with NCTSN university-based treatment development centers. For example, CTPI is currently working with the New York University Institute for the Study of Trauma Recovery Program on implementation of a treatment model for adolescent girls known as Life Skills/Life Story. It recently began an implementation of trauma systems therapy for children in foster care in New York City by drawing on expertise from the Center for Medical and Refugee Trauma at Boston University Medical Center. NCTSN membership provides CTPI with access to significant resources, including access to training on state-of-the-art trauma treatments, the opportunity for research collaboration with treatment model developers, and access to a web-based core data collection system for evaluation studies. Participation in a national network also introduces new levels of complexity and the additional demands that flow from inclusion in an independent, cross-site evaluation of the NCTSN program.

PRINCIPLES OF SUCCESS

Both the literature and agency experience indicate that academic researchers and service providers do not automatically see themselves as natural allies. Indeed, many observers have concluded that conducting research in community-based agencies is like mixing oil and water. They have also likened the process of getting potential partners on the same page to dating, to marriage, or to a "slow cooker"

(Currie et al., 2005). Consequently, prior to embarking on a collaborative research project it is critical that the players take the time needed to establish rapport and a cooperative relationship.

Given this reality, what makes for success? Community-based agencies often point to the need for a shared purpose, mandate, and problem definition, commitment to collaboration, capacity-building activities, and access to resources (Reback et al., 2002). However, in practice, the achievement of these desired outcomes depends on the ability of the partners to manage a variety of dynamic tensions that are always in motion.

That is, the partners have to learn to balance the following competing tensions: *(a)* institutional versus partnership priorities, *(b)* control versus compromise, *(c)* infrastructure versus project development, *(d)* collaborative versus independent activities, *(e)* building new capacity versus demanding more from existing capacity, *(f)* burden versus value, *(g)* pace of research versus pace of practice, *(h)* collaborative "dual citizenship" roles versus a primary institution role, and *(i)* change and innovation versus maintaining the status quo.

Partnership versus Institutional Research Priorities

The research–practitioner relationship can be easily undercut by the uneven level of research skills between the partners. Unless both parties buy into the research question, the community agency practitioner is likely to feel imposed upon by the project. Thus, it is generally agreed that actual research should not begin until both partners have worked together long enough to agree on the issue to be investigated (Galinsky, Turnbull, Meglin, & Wilner, 1993). At first glance this may seem easy, but tensions surrounding "whose question is it" may stymie the project unless the research question to be decided upon has meaning and value to each partner. To this end, the formulation of the research question must reflect and balance the priorities of both the partners and the joint project. Neither the researcher's question nor the practitioner's question can be regarded as "more important." Only a careful exploration of "what's in it for both parties" can ultimately neutralize the predisposition of the practitioners to feel that the researcher is imposing on them. It is generally agreed that viable partnerships result when the project addresses issues of essential interests to both parties. When that is the case, the resulting studies are more readily perceived as valuable, especially if they have a high use/need ratio (Saxe, 2006). One area of vital interest these days involves government and foundation expectations for outcomes evaluation. Although outcomes evaluation and field effectiveness studies are not perfectly aligned, beginning with outcomes has helped JBFCS to build the capacity to do more rigorous studies.

Control versus Compromise over Methodology

The question of research methodology also creates dynamic tensions that need to be balanced. Any hard-won consensus about a research question can quickly be undone when it comes to deciding "how the question will be answered." On the one hand, the rules of science require that researchers control the parameters of a study. That is, the research partner typically seeks a well-defined highly selected study population, as well as the use of focused and structured assessments and treatments, random assignment to treatment and control groups, and strict adherence to a manualized protocol (McKay, 2004).

On the other hand, clinical practice settings usually lack such control or it may appear to violate professional norms. Control may not be possible or may slip away as practitioners are pressed for time and expected to serve highly diverse and often multi-problem patients in an environment of dwindling resources that limits training, monitoring, and oversight. Professional norms also leave practitioners reluctant to select some clients for treatment and deprive others of available services.

The typical compromise involves using a research design that compares the selected intervention with standard "treatment as usual," rather than a design that excludes anyone from services. While this resolves the practitioner's ethical concerns about assignment to a "no treatment" group, it does not resolve who will provide the research intervention and how strict or flexible the implementation can be. These interacting concerns need to be revisited regularly by the partners in order to maintain an effective balance of interests. In addition, practitioners understandably are often unclear as to the focus of the study: is it the treatment method or their own clinical competence? Thus, poorly understood comparative designs can make them feel their work is under the microscope and will be found lacking (McKay, 2004).

Infrastructure versus Project Development

A third dynamic tension exists between the knowledge that early inclusion of practitioners in the design of the study increases the likelihood of a successful partnership (Israel et al., 2005) and the requirement of stakeholders, especially funding sources, that the research be clearly defined and the implementation plan be fully spelled out in order to receive the needed resources. This is a chicken and egg dilemma: Which comes first: the full development of a research design, or the securing of the funding needed to devote time to relationship building and creation of an infrastructure to carry out the project?

The tension is resolved when funding includes an open-ended planning phase to allow the researchers and the practitioners to define the research focus of the project, subject to later review by the funding source. Such planning enables each partner to contribute what he or she knows best, to clarify underlying assumptions, and to build mutual trust. The community agency partner provides his or her knowledge of clients, community, culture, and desired innovations. The researcher provides his or her knowledge of funding sources, grant writing and research design, and implementation (Lamb, Greenlick, & McCarty, 1998). Both partners contribute to the interpretation of the data. In addition to identifying the best contribution of each partner and promoting trust, the availability of such funded planning time allows the partners to work out key issues of mission, governance, and communication that if not very clear from the start can often interfere with ongoing collaboration.

Collaborative versus Independent Activities

Collaboration involves a willingness to work together and to devote time to development of a team committed to equal input. That is, the partners need to "click" so that they can stick it out when the going gets tough. To meet each other's needs, the partners need to take the time to understand and appreciate each other's strengths, weakness, foibles, sense of humor, and organizational constraints. However, a competing pull comes from the time needed for each player to continue to conduct business on the home front. The need to fulfill professional and organizational responsibility that exists outside of the collaboration may interfere with agreed upon meeting times, phone calls, and deadlines. Failure to acknowledge and respect that required absences and delays do not necessarily indicate a lack of commitment can produce corrosive "us vs. them" attitudes antithetical to team building.

This tension can be eased through leadership "buy-in" and open communication. Such buy-in opens the door to various types of support. Each partner's leadership can facilitate the collaboration by freeing members from noncritical organizational commitments; they can also communicate when this is not possible, which will help reduce misinterpretations. Leadership participation in the team's working meeting can promote communication and collaboration, especially when potential roadblocks occur.

Open communication goes beyond the usual practitioner/researcher team discussion to keeping all project staff fully informed of developments, providing feedback to clinical supervisors and administrative personnel, giving regular reports of issues, changes, and results; identifying clear boundaries regarding the ownership of the data produced by the research team; as well as deciding in advance how to determine the method by which credit and authorship of publications will be assigned (Reback et al., 2002).

Other expressions of leadership buy-in that can support increased collaboration include helping frontline clinicians, who demonstrate research proclivities to obtain small grants that fund pilot projects of their own and offering seminars and feedback sessions on topics related to the project, if the clinicians do not need to be blind to the results.

Building New Capacity versus Demanding More from Existing Capacity

Both researchers and practitioners share the necessary desire to expand and improve the quality of treatment and prevention services for those in need by engaging in research. But from the practitioner's perspective, each person's capacity—or the use of their time—must be settled prior to the inception of a study. For frontline clinicians the question is, Will I be released from clinical responsibilities to perform research duties, or will the research task be added to my already-demanding regular work?

One way to manage this tension is to use research funds to spread the workload by paying for the time of additional practitioner(s) to work on the project. Another is to fund a separate research team to work in the agency. Both remedies require constant monitoring of both the practice and the research implementation. In addition, someone is needed—preferably an on-site dedicated project manager—to oversee pragmatic details such as subject recruitment/informed consent, data collection/data completeness, and supervision of the intervention.

The simultaneous dissemination of new evidence-based treatments while subjecting them to field effectiveness studies is another important priority for research partnerships. The capacity-building challenge it creates can turn into a serious impediment to the progress of the partnership. The community partner experiences this issue most acutely because in order to do the study, he or she must find the means to first build the capacity to provide and supervise the new approach. The need to release staff from income-generating activities to gain this new knowledge creates a severe tension for most real-world clinical service providers who face constant time and income pressures generated by current funding policies in community-based mental health. These pressures make it harder for program administrators and frontline staff to perceive the training and new skills as something that adds value rather than something that creates new burdens. While this training is a crucial precondition for any field effectiveness study, most research budgets do not include funds to build this necessary capacity. In the final analysis, in light of new mandates to implement evidence-based treatment, the adoption of new evidence-based practices by community-based agencies will require some kind of fiscal incentive.

Burden versus Value to the Agency

This dimension of dynamic tension refers to the impact of additional activities and the presence of new people in a community-based program. Cooperation between the clinical site and the research team inevitably places demands on the site's administrative staff. The demands on the clinical staff vary widely depending on whether the research requires clinicians to be the primary data gatherers or whether the project brings in its own research staff.

One's location in the hierarchy of a large, multi-level agency may also shape the perception of the "value" of engaging in research. Top agency leadership may find the creation of new knowledge as a way to enhance the agency's public reputation and therefore worth the extra burden. In contrast, the leadership of the division "hosting" the research as well as the division's program directors and staff may look for more immediate value for ongoing daily practice. If neither the administrative nor clinical staff at the project site understands the study's potential practice utility, the less tangible burdens placed on them will not be counterbalanced by a sense of the project's value. Instead, they may conclude that the study's only utility is for building an empirical base for research (McKay, 2004).

To mediate the burden, program administrators and clinicians must ensure that the clinic staff and patients understand the purpose and presence of the study. This is vital to both gaining support for the study and to securing accurate answers to patients' questions. Time-consuming practical interactions are also necessary to allow researchers to learn clinical routines, locate records, maintain project procedures, and to allow the administrative staff to know the research team's schedule, take their phone calls, find office space, and contact patients.

Pace of Research versus Pace of Practice

Successful field research often hinges on the willingness to include practitioner input on how to adapt protocols to fit site-specific clinician and client variables. However, practitioners are often not aware that an institutional review board (IRB) operates like a silent partner in this process, necessitating multiple layers of approval for any design changes intended to balance time, burden, and value arrived at by partnership consensus. IRB alterations of the shared design to ensure the protection of human subjects often slows the pace of the research project and can affect access to its findings. Practitioners who struggle on a daily basis with problems that need immediate responses often find the resulting slowdown in the timetable incomprehensible and frustrating. Researchers, on the other hand, are frustrated by the clinician's desire to get answers quickly from a single study when the researchers know that multiple studies may be necessary before definitive results are available (Reback et al., 2002).

Once a project is started, real-world clinical time issues related to subject recruitment intrude. Researchers often feel that clinicians do not move quickly enough to find subjects. However, the researchers need to understand that the pace is affected by more than "no shows" or refusals to participate. The shortage of clients that meet inclusion criteria is because the actual flow through of clients may be much less than overall caseload statistics would indicate, making it crucial to recruit all potential subjects. However, in the fray of demanding schedules clinicians often need regular prompts to ensure that they do not miss cases due to a failure to remember the inclusion criteria.

Collaborative "Dual Citizenship" Role versus Primary Institution Role

Complex social systems often define members as "insiders" and erect barriers to perceived "outsiders." Steps that lower these "immune system" responses within the partner's institutions can help to promote the integration necessary for ultimate success of the alliance (Lefley & Bestman, 1991). These steps may include a reciprocal appointment procedure whereby agency partners receive faculty appointments and academic partners receive agency teaching appointments. In addition, the project can make sure that meetings and other activities occur on an equal basis at both institutions, which has the advantage of allowing greater opportunity for project and non-project staff to relate to one another.

The creation of such "dual citizenship" as clinician/ researcher eases the tension for the participants by increasing the visibility, familiarity, and acceptance of each partner at the other partner's institution. This can also help the partners develop the role of "culture broker" in which they represent the views of the other party to the home institution (Lefley & Bestman, 1991). The potential risk here is that the person may come to be perceived as becoming too closely allied with the other institution.

Change versus Maintaining the Status Quo

Successful partnerships involve responding to larger system pressures to innovate and change. This need for change may conflict with the need to fulfill regulatory obligations and productivity standards, both of which call for business as usual. The constant fiscal pressures resulting from the continuing underfunding of mental health services also pushes the system toward maintaining the status quo.

Upcoming regulatory changes may well decrease the distance between making changes and maintaining the status quo. As new expectations from government and the private sector link third-party payments to evidence of efficacy, the viability and quality of the service program will become an ultimate shared "vital interest" shared by clinicians and researchers. The new mandates promise to increase the demand for research and practice partnerships, but obstacles that stand in their way must be reduced by attending to the real costs of such a transition.

OBSTACLES TO COLLABORATION

Individual practitioner factors and features of the larger organizational system may present obstacles to collaboration that differ from those already described as interfering with the development of a research–practitioner partnership. Collaboration may be stalled as well by the clinician's beliefs about treatment, negative attitudes toward research, and lack of knowledge about evidence-based practice.

Clinicians often believe that therapy is an art and not a science, that it cannot be measured, that the protocol under study is too rigid and narrow, that most cases are too complicated and will not benefit from using such tools, and that studying practice could be harmful to one's professional discipline (Weisz et al., 1998). As for research, clinicians may dislike the need for the rigid control of treatment conditions, constant monitoring of their practice, the complexity of research articles, the difficulty interpreting findings, and what they perceive as the researchers concern about the need for "scientific" data rather than the needs of people.

Partnership efforts to promote adoption of new evidence-based treatments must contend with the lack of practitioners with the skills and knowledge needed to provide trauma-informed evidence-based treatment. This situation reflects insufficient attention to evidence-based treatment and other trauma treatment methods in professional education, which often continues to focus on conceptually appealing, personal theoretical orientations the lack of opportunities for hands-on experience with evidence-based treatment in student internships, and the limited number of agencies using such practices (Citizens' Committee for Children, 2002).

Obstacles at the organizational level cluster around issues of funding and reimbursement, lack of organizational role models, and supervisory and administrative resources. Dependent on outside funding and reimbursement, community-based organizations may find it difficult to become interested in or to find the time or resources needed to incorporate outcomes evaluation and/or new treatment models. Indeed, insurance plans typically pay only for face-to-face contacts, leaving clinical services additionally pressed by the need to absorb the costs of all the non-face-to-face activities required to manage complex cases. They rarely underwrite time-consuming training or the restructuring of services, even when the changes are needed to adopt practices they mandate, such as evidence-based treatment. The reimbursement systems also lack fiscal incentives that link clinical income to improved outcomes or use of newer efficacious treatments (Citizens' Committee for Children, 2002).

Since the lessons learned thus far from trauma-informed practice and evaluation are not well integrated into the wider mental health system and consequently into individual practice sites, young clinicians do not have ready access to early adopters of innovation to serve as role models of evidence-based treatment trained clinical supervisors. This deficiency in organizational and administrative resources reflects the lack of outcomes research and a bias against it, and the limitations of existing outcomes research, as well as a lack of administrative program resources. These include training, marketing, clinical-decision-making aides to promote integration of evidence-based treatments, and parent engagement strategies (Wilson & Saunders, 2006).

STRATEGIES FOR IMPROVEMENT

The highly desired formation of practitioner–research partnerships and sustaining their productivity over the long term remains challenging. Over the past 40 years JBFCS has tried three major approaches to foster practice and field effectiveness research. Looking at these can offer some ideas about the advantages and disadvantages of each way of conducting research in a community-based agency. No one approach eliminates all of the dilemmas, but some hold more promise than the others for bridging the gap between researchers and practitioners.

The following possible strategies may create opportunities for success. The key steps include *(a)* sustaining an internal commitment to research; *(b)* emphasizing process over product; *(c)* creating a lasting infrastructure rather than relying solely on ongoing projects; *(d)* budgeting that reflects "real costs"; *(e)* attending consistently to expectations; *(f)* expanding the partnership to include community participation; *(g)* evaluating the impact of the partnership on the practitioner organization; and *(h)* use of a systematic implementation model.

Maintaining an Internal Commitment to Research

The definition of maintaining an internal commitment to research needs to be broadened beyond the usual emphasis on product. To this end, the agency must value research and sustain an interest and a commitment to it even when no research projects are operative. That is, the agency must create and maintain a research-compatible environment. The creation of such a "research-friendly culture" within a service organization includes advocating the value of reflection on practice, supporting data collection and use, promoting the value of a learning organization, and comfort with the needed ongoing organizational change (Tobin & Hickie, 1998).

The top leaders of JBFCS have consistently valued the role of research in promoting a culture of self-reflection within the agency. This has culminated in the agency's current investment in the collaborative process, which allows it to *(a)* help develop individual research-oriented clinicians, which has the potential to create a critical mass of research receptivity; *(b)* support internal research champions within both senior and middle management to serve as role models of "dual identity" change agents; *(c)* provide released time to staff to pursue research interests; *(d)* endorse small seed grants from the CSSWP; *(e)* support the acquisition of advanced degrees by frontline clinical staff; and *(f)* create an endowed Education Institute at the agency that promotes continuing professional education and the maintenance of a "learning organization" stance. This type of agency support acts to "detoxify" research, but it is highly dependent on individuals. Thus, acceptance of the role of research does not automatically generalize to the whole system because of the agency's high service commitments. It requires constant attention to finding the proper balance between time devoted to research and time devoted to program management and service provision.

Emphasizing Process over Product

Successful agency–university partnerships also depend on establishing processes to correct the often unspoken perception held by the university partner—and perhaps the agency partner as well—that research findings are a more valid form of new knowledge than practice wisdom, and therefore research and researchers carry more weight and prestige than practice and practitioners. Even if these attitudes remain beneath the surface, their latent presence must be anticipated by the partners if they hope to secure the practitioner's cooperation with data collection. In the end the routine collection and use of data requires compromise on both sides.

More specifically, clinicians can be helped to counteract their almost automatic "default" tendency to challenge the collection of data because they fear it might reveal problems with their work. To this end, the data collection can be reframed as a way to assess the effectiveness of the treatment procedures rather than the skillfulness of the provider. It also helps if the agency or the research project includes activities that help clinicians improve their data analysis skills. To address the burden that data collection places on agency workers, whenever possible, agencies can make data collection instruments part of standard clinical record keeping. From their side, researchers need to develop a tolerance for the natural imperfections of agency-based data. This includes a willingness to relinquish the desire to secure only data of publishable "research grade" (McKay et al., 2004).

Creation of a Lasting Infrastructure

The creation of a lasting infrastructure is still another component of success. This often boils down to available resources. Research budgets typically cover items directly related to project implementation, which often excludes the "real costs" to the agency. Critical underfunded items include the cost in time and money involved in *(a)* training and supervising clinicians who are asked to use new treatment methods, and *(b)* providing the clerical and administrative support personnel needed to absorb the additional work generated by the administration of project protocols. While funding sources may presuppose these supports as in-kind contributions from the sponsoring agency, in fact they drain already hard-pressed agency budgets. In the final analysis, the success of agency-based research rests on being able to shift from project-based funding to the creation of an appropriately funded lasting infrastructure that can sustain new partner relationships overtime.

Attending to Expectations

Expectations can also influence success. Agencies need to recognize that comfort with ongoing organizational change includes acknowledging that "the difficulties inherent in the practice–research partnership must be treated as an expected part of the process so that practitioners and researchers are aware of and not overwhelmed by the problems that can develop" (Galinsky et al., 1993). Expected difficulties can include not properly estimating the complexity of the tasks being undertaken; expecting "success" on the first try; and/or having major components of project rollout get out of synch, either because of technological delays or a prolonged IRB approval process. Defining as many expectations as possible in advance permits the planned activities needed to support a sustained research climate.

Inclusion of the Community

Another very critical success factor involves making the community a partner in the necessary and challenging creation of the practitioner–research partnership from the outset. However, agencies and universities alone do not have the knowledge as to what does and does not work. Projects are more successful if the community partner is involved in setting the goals of the research, planning its design, and interpreting the results. However, for each project "the community" must be clearly defined (Hoagwood, Burns, & Weisz, 2002; McKay et al., 2004). Does it mean interacting with the residents of a discrete geographical area or the consumers of a particular service agency, who may or may not be a part of the partnership?

Regardless of the definition used, most of the literature describes partnerships primarily between academics and community residents rather than three-way academic /community-based agency/community resident partnerships. In contrast, Chapter Two by Mary McKay (in this volume) extends the notion of collaboration to include research in "action" with consumers, family members, providers, systems, and communities. Her comprehensive approach focuses attention on the added value that results from making inclusion of "the community" central to the conduct of research.

Evaluating a Partnership's Impact on the Practitioner's Organization

Despite the substantial attention to the creation of practitioner–researcher partnerships, few attempts have been made to evaluate the impact of implementing a partnership on the practitioner organization. Fortunately, King et al. (2005) have created a tool to measure the "community impacts of research oriented partnerships (CIROP) in the health and social services." Designed to be applicable to a broad array of potential researchers and collaborators, the CIROP captures perceptions of midterm impact in the areas of knowledge enhancement, research skill enhancement, and information use. The developers of this tool have pilot studies underway to collect evidence of its psychometric properties.

Use of a Systematic Implementation Model

How does one translate the results gained from effective partnerships into prompt implementation of research findings? The delay in moving "science to service" has been a continuing frustration (National Advisory Mental Health Council, 1999). Although numerous stumbling blocks to dissemination, adoption, and adaptation of results remain, partnerships can draw on recommended comprehensive conceptual frameworks and well-developed models that show how to systematically move newly developed services into use in the very practice settings where they were developed. For example, Glisson and his team at the university of Tennessee developed a model of organizational and community intervention to support the improvement of social and mental health services for children (Glisson & Schoenwald, 2005). Called Availability, Responsiveness, and Continuity (ARC) it "incorporates intervention components from organizational development, inter-organizational domain development, the diffusion of innovation, and technology transfer that target social, strategic, and technological factors in effective children's services."

Hoagwood et al's Clinic/Community Intervention Development Model (CID) even more explicitly connects research to practice (Hoagwood et al., 2002). CID is an eight-step conceptual framework "designed to accelerate the pace at which the science base for mental health services can be developed, adapted, refined, and taken to scale in a variety of practice settings or communities. The model outlines a series of steps that begin and end with the practice setting (e.g., clinic, school, health center, etc.) where the treatment or service will ultimately be delivered." It describes the "scientific phases for developing treatments or services for children's mental health problems—from manual development to wide-scale dissemination—with the goal of ensuring that the end product—a scientifically valid treatment or service—will be grounded, useable, and relevant to the practice context for which it is ultimately intended." It also extends the model to the dissemination and implementation of the intervention into a variety of practice settings or communities.

Despite the complexity of the task, Hoagwood et al. conclude that "complacency is not an option. Creating a usable science of children's mental health services requires constant attention to the factors that may undercut or diminish their impact, and persistent focus on understanding why and under what conditions such services can *attain* their intended outcomes and can be *sustained* within communities."

This community provider's perspective on research partnerships demonstrates that while JBFCS has avoided complacency by shifting from an isolated research department toward full collaboration with academic partners many challenges remain. Adoption and diffusion of new methods throughout all levels of the agency and simultaneous adaptation based on field effectiveness studies necessitates a willingness to function with the ongoing tensions described. Striking a balance between the continual struggle with obstacles and tensions stimulated by change and the benefits derived from it requires that a learning environment is fostered and maintained.

Acknowledgments. This work was supported by grant 15SM54267-03 from the Substance Abuse and Mental Health Administration and a National Institute of Mental Health grant 1R24MH63910-01A1. Robert Abramovitz was formerly affiliated with the Jewish Board of Family and Children's Services. The authors wish to acknowledge the contribution of their colleagues Rick Greenberg, PhD, Bruce Grellong, PhD, Paula Panzer, MD, Claude Chemtob, PhD, and Jeffrey Newcorn, MD, for their valuable contributions to this chapter.

References

Citizens' Committee for Children. (2002). *Paving the way: New directions for children's mental health treatment services.* New York: Author.

Currie, M., King, G., Rosenbaum, P., Law, M., Kertoy, M., & Specht, J. (2005). A model of impacts of research partnerships in health and social services. *Evaluation and Program Planning, 28,* 400–412.

Galinsky, M. J., Turnbull, J. E., Meglin, D. E., & Wilner, M. E. (1993). Confronting the reality of collaborative practice research: Issues of practice, design, measurement, and team development. *Social Work, 38*(4), 440–449.

Glisson, C., & Schoenwald, S. K. (2005). The ARC organizational and community intervention strategy for implementing evidence-based children's mental health treatments. *Mental Health Services Research, 7*(4), 243-259.

Guterman, N. B., & Cameron, M. (1997). Assessing the impact of community violence on children and youths. *Social Work, 42*(5), 495–505.

Hoagwood, K., Burns, B. J., & Weisz, J. (2002). A profitable conjunction: From science to service in children's mental health. In *Community-based interventions for youth with severe emotional disturbances,* edited by B. J. Burns & K. Hoagwood. New York: Oxford University Press.

Institute of Medicine. (2001). *Crossing the quality chasm: A new health system for the 21st century.* Washington, DC: Author.

Israel, B., Parker, E., Rowe, Z., Salvatore, A., Minkler, M., López, J., et al. (2005). Community-based participatory research: Lessons learned from the Centers for Children's Environmental Health and Disease Prevention Research. *Environmental Health Perspectives, 113*(10), 1463–1471.

Jenkins, S. (1990). "*The center concept*". Paper presented at the Conference on Research Utilization, Michigan.

King, G., Servais, M., Currie, M., Kertoy, M., Law, M., Rosenbaum, P., et al. (2005). *A measure of community impacts of research-orientedpartnerships (CIROP).*

Lamb, S., Greenlick, M., & McCarty, D. (1998). *Bridging the gap between practice and research: Forging partnerships with community-based drug and alcohol treatment.* Washington, DC: The National Academy Press.

Lefley, H. P., & Bestman, E. W. (1991). Public-academic linkages for culturally sensitive community mental health. *Community Mental Health Journal, 27*(6), 473–478

McKay, M. M., Hibbert, R., Hoagwood, K., Rodriguez, J., Murray, L., Legerski, J., & Fernandez, D. (2004). Integrating evidence-based engagement interventions into "real world" child mental health settings. *Brief Treatment and Crisis Intervention, 4*(2), 177–186.

Mullen, E. J. (1998). Linking the university and a social agency in collaborative research: Principles and examples. *Scandinavian Journal of Social Welfare, 7,* 152–158.

National Advisory Mental Health Council's Clinical Treatment and Services Research Workgroup. (1999). *Bridging science and service: A report* of the National Advisory Mental Health Council's Clinical Treatment and Services Research Work Group. Rockville, MD: National Advisory Mental Health Council.

Polsky, H. W. (1962). *Cottage six: The social system of delinquent boys in residential treatment.* New York: Russell Sage Foundation.

Reback, C. J., Cohen, A. J., Freese, T. E., & Shoptaw, S. (2002). Making collaboration work: Key components of practice/research partnerships. *Journal of Drug Issues, 32*(3), 837–848.

Rivard, J. C., Bloom, S., Abramovitz, R., Pasquale, L., Duncan, M., McCorckle. D., & Gelman, A. (2003). Assessing the implementation and effects of a trauma-focused intervention for youths in residential treatment. *Psychiatric Quarterly, 74*(2),,137–154.

Saxe, G. (2006). *Bringing the evidence-base to evidence-based treatments: User centered mental health interventions and service.* Unpublished manuscript.

Tobin, M., & Hickie, I. (1998). Outcomes focused service delivery: Developing an academic-management partnership. *Australian and New Zealand Journal of Psychiatry 33*(3), 327-336.

U.S. Public Health Service Office of the Surgeon General. (1999). *Mental health: A report of the Surgeon General.* Rockville, MD: U.S. Department of Health and Human Services.

Weisz, J. R., Donenberg, G. H., Susan S., & Weiss, B. (1995). Bridging the gap between laboratory and clinic in child and adolescent psychotherapy. *Journal of Consulting and Clinical Psychology, American Psychological Association, 63*(5), 688–701.

Weisz, J., Huey, S., & Weersing, V. (1998). Psychotherapy outcome research with children and adolescents. *Advances in Clinical Child Psychology,* 20, 49-91.

Wilson, C., & Saunders, B. E. (2006). Exploring alternative strategies for diffusion of best practice. Retrieved on August 1, 2009, from http://www.musc.edu/cvc.

Chapter Five

Creative Community Collaborations:
A Research Casebook and Toolkit

Robin Peth Pierce, Serene Olin, Kimberly Eaton Hoagwood, and Peter Jensen

Collaborative community research is not for everyone. Some researchers prefer to be lone rangers, effecting social change single-handedly, in consort only with their conscience. Some are uninterested in questions of social change altogether. But the history of social policy in this country suggests that the social changes that have had the most traction and long-lasting impact have been those that united disparate parties, perspectives, and persons, and identified a common ground for change. In short, collaborative research can promote change by advancing a strong and self-correcting scientific agenda.

In the field of children's mental health, significant scientific breakthroughs have resulted in the creation of a robust, yet still new knowledge base on the promotion of mental health and treatment of mental disorders. The scientific discoveries of the last 25 years have improved the lives of literally millions of children and families in diverse communities throughout this country. While this new knowledge is an important first step, no complementary set of skills exists on how best to embed these services in communities, or how to work with communities to ensure that knowledge is put into practice. In fact, the majority of the advances in the field have arisen from studies conducted in relative isolation from the communities and contexts in which they are to be implemented. This has engendered some distrust of the research enterprise altogether.

Other significant research challenges include people's perception that researchers are serving their own goals, conducting "hit and run" research that will leave communities in the lurch. These research challenges are confounded by the fact that there is limited graduate training on conducting collaborative community research. Of the approximately 800 psychology programs in the United States, only about 75 offer a program in community psychology (Council of Program Directors in Community Research and Action, 2001). It is one purpose of this book to provide examples of research methods and approaches that

89

explicitly attend to the context of communities. This is what we mean by collaboration.

Throughout this book, the authors have illustrated how conducting collaborative research is a creative process—a process which is transactional and fluid, with constant give and take, and on-the-job training. The dynamic nature of this work, the need for incorporating the practical realities of each community's needs, and the constant engagement with those in the community require that one enter into collaborations carefully, equipped with the tools to conduct such research. As such, this chapter serves as both a casebook of examples and a "toolkit" of specific steps to guide the development of community collaborations. It also recaps the key principles of collaboration outlined in Chapters Two, Three and Four of this book.

Collaboration is not a panacea—and may not even be possible in certain situations, especially where time and money are limited. First, the timeline generally includes at least 1 year prior to the planned recruitment for a study, since much work is done during this period building trust and relationships within the community. Second, acknowledging the limitations of the funding source(s) and making the budgeting process transparent are essential ingredients of any successful community collaboration. Building strong relationships with community partners often requires twice the cost originally estimated. And while a study design depends on study goals, major funding sources typically award grants for a hypothesis that has already been generated; in community collaborations, the development of the hypothesis is done only after substantial time and effort have already been invested into the community. Options for financing collaborative efforts are limited but may include both traditional research grants and private sources, such as foundations.

Another essential ingredient to successful collaborative community research, often underestimated, is the need for researchers to possess a personality that can meet the demands of collaborative work. While researchers need not be a cross between Mother Theresa and Albert Einstein, the demanding nature of this work calls for both cognitive and social passion with large doses of humility thrown in for good measure.[1] Finely tuned interpersonal skills are needed for the community collaborator who must sometimes act as a teacher, coach, and cheerleader. The community collaborator should also be willing to learn-and to recognize, appreciate, and respect the knowledge that all partners bring to the table. As in any field, personalities best suited for this type of research are those who have a good tolerance for ambiguity, who do not need public recognition, and who are flexible in their beliefs and methods.

Traditional research has placed a premium on and rewarded independence. In contrast, collaborative community research emphasizes the notion of engaging others, with the goal of making a greater contribution to the human condition.[2] We believe that this partnership also leads to a stronger science. True hand-in-hand work with communities, including the development of treatments and programs that are sustainable, will not only better meet the mental heath needs of children but also strengthen the communities in which children and their families live. In the field of child and adolescent mental health, this process of collaboration is less-often studied and reported upon. This toolkit and casebook are an attempt to crystallize the process of collaboration, and they provide examples of how researchers have dealt with the particular problems that have arisen in the course of their work in communities.

CASEBOOK AND TOOLKIT FOR CONDUCTING COLLABORATIVE COMMUNITY RESEARCH

Precollaboration Work

Defining the "Community"
Before collaboration can begin, researchers can identify the key partners from the community with whom they will collaborate. Much like learning to ride a bike without training wheels, researchers need to feel out the ground under their feet and learn about the community in which they will work, including potential partners. A community is not simply a geographical boundary that divides one town from the next, one county from another; it is made of people. The definition of a "community" is situational, shifting within the context of the issue or problem under discussion. Community can be defined not only by demographics but also by religion, political party, and other affiliations. There are several ways to learn more about a community: by attending community meetings, hosting community forums, conducting focus groups with key stakeholders or informants, or conducting a needs assessment.

Attend community meetings.   Attend community meetings, such as school board, township, or city government meetings. Listening in on these meetings will paint a picture of the community's landscape, providing insight into community leadership and historical, as well as current, issues.

Host a public forum.   Another effective way to learn more about a community is to become a resource to the community. Bring to them knowledge and training in your area of expertise, freely and generously, with no strings attached. The tone of this initial outreach sets the stage for future collaborations, and it should not be one in which quick answers to problems are offered; researchers should not enter communities with hypotheses already in hand. Hosting a public forum (e.g., town-hall meeting) allows researchers to understand a community's vision of their most pressing problems and issues.

Getting a Community Ready for Research
After clearly defining a community, researchers should work to get a community ready for research. This requires the identification of key leaders within the community and an assessment of community issues.

Find a champion.   Communities ready for research often have a "champion" who is willing to spearhead the effort. In most cases, having local "buy-in" before the research is undertaken makes for smoother implementation. Communities ready for research have leaders committed to improving the problem at hand, and even more broadly, have the political support needed to ensure that adequate resources will be available for the financial stability of the project.

Conduct a needs assessment.   Each community has different needs. As a companion to setting up advisory boards and assessing political support, an initial formal assessment, done with the input of the community, will help flesh out community problems and issues. It is hard when the community is divided on what the real issues or problems are—unity on goals and priorities needs to be established. In some cases, researchers have set up collaborative research projects only to find out halfway through the process that few potential participants existed in the community. For example, in one collaboration, both researchers and community leaders were in agreement that a preventive prenatal program would greatly benefit women and children in their community; however, an initial assessment found few qualified participants (e.g., in this case, mothers at less than 28 weeks of gestation) did not exist in their community.[3] This needs assessment phase, which will likely involve gathering data from a variety of community organizations, can also serve to identify potential sources of funding for the planned intervention.

Getting Research Ready for a Community
Getting research ready for a community requires juggling many duties at once. The list of actions below, while not exhaustive, includes some basic steps to get research ready for a community.

Creating advisory/collaborative boards.   To create advisory boards, pull together community leaders in an on-the-ground grassroots effort. Potential members are those from economic, social, and educational organizations, including but not limited to schools, religious organizations, service/citizen groups (e.g., rotary clubs), and the business community (e.g., local business networking groups), state policy makers, advocates/parents, or consumers. These boards serve as a forum for organizing the key stakeholders in the community and offer the opportunity to formalize the communities' involvement in the research effort. Initial conversations with the community help to answer such questions as:[4]

- What is the nature of the mental health issue or problem?
- What does it mean to be involved in the study?
- Is the population appropriate?

The answers to these questions gauge the feasibility of a study *before* researchers undergo the time-consuming, costly process of grant writing.

Consider a pilot study to determine the feasibility of the study.   Conducting a pilot study helps to prevent a potential waste of time and resources; in many cases, grants have been awarded only to determine, post award, that eligible participants could not be identified. Consider a pilot phase of at least a year, even if data on the efficacy of the intervention already exists.

Allow and schedule enough time for the site development process.   A thorough and lengthy precollaboration process will help to determine whether a potential community is a good fit. An adequate site development process will allow time for potential problems to surface, and it will give researchers time to tackle these early on. For example, a change in community leadership can result in the termination of programs or policies, thereby affecting study recruitment.

Prepare a draft of all technical assistance and training materials up front, even though they may not be needed then, and seek community input.   For some interventions, dissemination materials may be needed up front; for others, the materials will have to be modified or tailored for particular community needs once the research project is underway. Preparing a draft of materials as soon as possible provides a chance to get early community feedback and to revise materials before dissemination.

Determine the cost of the collaboration and ensure that resources can be available.   Adequate funding is essential to a successful collaboration. Accurately assessing the cost of delivering a program or treatment will prevent monetary shortfalls and avoid the possibility of having to terminate the intervention halfway through. In addition, include costs for evaluation of the intervention up front; often, communities are less willing to budget for evaluation costs, but the importance of the evaluation should be stressed early on.

Negotiate the "degree" of intervention flexibility up front.   While flexibility often depends on the phase of research and stated study goals (e.g., testing efficacy vs. effectiveness), the acceptable "leeway" in the study should be clearly defined—and palatable to the community. Which aspects of the intervention or program are nonnegotiable? Which are negotiable?

Help the community see the value in the program.   Show the community what the research can do. For example, if the intervention under study has already produced positive outcomes in other communities, elaborate on how the intervention worked in that community, and for whom. Researchers can perhaps help the community figure out how best to identify youth for whom the potential program might work, and propose other strategies for those who would not benefit. By providing a model for communities of how best to use their resources at hand, communities can better understand what they can get for their investment in the project.

Help the community own the model.   A true collaboration is one in which communities have a chance to provide input on the questions asked and solutions offered. Seeking and integrating their suggestions, whether via public forums or personal meetings, will help the community "own" the research, thereby increasing the collaboration's chance of success.

Do not overpromise.   The proposed research should not be presented as "the answer to all the problems" in the community. Be realistic with the community about the potential for positive outcomes, and present, in lay language, results of any efficacy studies (if applicable) to demonstrate the success of the program in other communities. Clearly delineate the potential outcomes.

Identify real and potential constraints of the collaboration.   List all of the known constraints that might impede the success of the collaboration. Some common constraints include community issues (e.g., current politics or policies) and research issues (e.g., the palatability of a randomized trial to the community). Brainstorm with the community to develop potential solutions to the problems.

Key Principles of Collaboration

Developing Shared Goals
Find common ground.   In the precollaboration phase, potential community partners are identified and convened. The next step is identifying and creating mutual self-interest. An example of this is in Oregon,[5] where researchers wanted to write a grant to incorporate teaching educators how best to manage behavior problems. Recent changes in state requirements to focus on behavior management for teacher education programs presented an opportunity for collaboration. While the modification of an educational curriculum is generally not feasible, in this case, it was in the mutual interest of both the researcher and the community to improve the teacher education program. Often, collaboration springs from an opportunity that initially presents itself as a problem in the community.

Make sure that you are on the "same page."   Researchers and community leaders bring different perspectives to the table. Often, there is a discrepancy between the health problems as defined by community and the researcher. What a trained epidemiologist sees looking at statistics on paper is different from what community leaders perceive as they look out across their community. For example, community leaders may cite violence as a key problem, while researchers may identify the risk factors for heart disease as the number-one killer in the community.[6] Researchers need to look for a common denominator in discussions with the community.

Recognize that "who" is brought into the collaboration influences the issues raised– and the questions asked and answered.   The process of identifying who is—and is not at the table—can uncover potential hidden agendas and politics. Does the balance at the table seem even? Are all of the voices and opinions being heard?

"Building trust is a "test of fire" and is never-ending. It requires the willingness to get unreasonably stood up and sometimes badly treated. In other words, getting stood up and coming back is one of the tests, along with constantly proving the worth of the program to new members."

Dr. Helen Kivnick,
director of CitySongs

Building Trust

Trust is the foundation of any collaborative project and, above all else, may make or break a project. If there is trust, the many problems and issues that may surface throughout the collaborative effort may be overcome. Both the researcher and community members should be honest and candid about expectations for the project. Researchers should make themselves available to the community, giving residents ample time and opportunity to "check them out." In some cases, researchers have also used intermediaries, organizations, or leaders well-known or accepted in the community to help establish trust and build a bridge to the community in which they wish to work.

Recognizing the Skills and Expertise of Community Partners

uccessful collaboration requires researchers to become very familiar with the resources available in the community, including the knowledge and expertise that community partners can bring. Some of these include the following:

- Sensitizing researchers to community needs
- Helping redirect research questions to increase relevance to community
- Providing access to the community in terms of recruitment and retention
- Possessing knowledge of community contextual issues and credibility
- Providing early feedback on study design and community attitudes
- Distinguishing consumers of services from advocates
- Building capacity at the local sites to sustain programs, post intervention
- Understanding the child/family history

"Often, more than the university investigator, the community partner can serve as a watchdog to ensure that the chosen study strategies are able to generate meaningful and potentially generalizable findings."

Dr. Mary McKay; see Chapter Two

Step by step, researchers can involve the community in every phase of the study, from precollaboration activities through recruitment and evaluation, to create effective, contextually appropriate interventions. Following are some examples of tangible ways researchers can involve communities in each step of the research process.[7]

Stage 1. Precollaboration.   Meet with the community to present the research idea even before writing a grant. Community members, including public-health professionals, potential study participants, and community advisory boards, provide vital information that can help shape the study.

Stage 2. Grant writing.   Go back to the community after a draft of the grant is written and have them review the draft before submitting the grant for review.

Stage 3. Start-up.   After the grant is received, conduct a small pilot study in the community.

Stage 4. Design of the intervention.   Hold focus groups to assess and revise the design of study, based on community and staff input. Include data from the pilot study to assess face validity and ensure that the intervention is a good fit with the community. While assessments of instruments and interventions are rarely done before interventions are deployed (often because little funding is available), community input needs to be integrated into the design if interventions are to be effective. One way to do this is to hire research staff from the community.

Stage 5. Recruitment.   Use data from the pilot study and focus groups, or seek additional community input on the best recruitment practices to help increase chances of successful recruitment.

Clarifying Working Assumptions
At the outset of the collaboration, researchers and community partners need to clearly explain and identify the assumptions under which they are operating. These assumptions center on things that matter most to communities, including privacy, the exploitation of the community in general, and control of money and other resources. In addition, a mission statement of the proposed collaboration can be drafted (see McKay, Chapter Two, this volume). Some examples of other sensitive issues for discussion include the following:[8]

- Discuss how papers that result from the project will be structured (e.g., as problem-oriented, defining the factors that contribute to the problems in the community vs. an "ain't it awful" paper).
- Discuss whether the study community should ever be compared to other communities.

"Language can shape and sometimes limit collaboration. As researchers, we struggled to find terms that communicated our belief that everyone on the research team, including family and community members, brings ideas, experiences, and expertise that are valuable to the research process."

Nancy Koroloff,
Chapter Three

- Discuss how disagreements on data/findings will be handled (e.g., requests to suppress findings).
- Discuss issues of data ownership (e.g., data are owned by the community; if the researcher dies or retires or leaves, data return to the community and are not accessible to graduate students or anyone else thereafter).
- Discuss how information generated by the collaborative effort will be handled (e.g., community-level or individual-level information will be kept private).
- Discuss the parameters of publication of findings beyond reporting immediate study findings in journal articles (e.g., the publication of a book for profit, and if so, addressing concerns such as exploitation and royalty generation).
- Discuss monetary compensation and other money issues (e.g., who controls the resources).

Developing a Common Language and Regular Opportunities for Communication

In any collaboration, many people come together with good intentions, but with very diverse backgrounds and perspectives, often leaving the group without a "common language." If collaborations are to be more successful, a common language should be developed that both the community and the researchers can relate to and understand.[9] In most cases, developing a common language will help communities engage more fully in a collaborative process. Researchers have a wealth of academic knowledge about the etiology of mental health disorders, and therefore speak and write in academic terms—terms the average community member does not use. For example, the term "at risk," while appropriate to describe segments of a population in a professional medical journal, can be misinterpreted by the community. Other words, such as "diagnosis" are not family- or patient-friendly terms because they label rather than describe. Thus, the many "languages" spoken in any collaboration may derail efforts.

Why Collaboration?

Collaboration with key community constituents has been described as necessary to: *(1)* enhance relevance of research questions; *(2)* develop research procedures that are acceptable to potential participants; *(3)* address obstacles to conducting community-based research activities; *(4)* maximize usefulness of research findings; and *(5)* expand community-level resources to sustain youth-focused intervention and prevention programs beyond research or demonstration funding.

(Mary McKay and The Chans Board)

In many cases, the use of a public-health approach and language—identifying a community's strengths and weaknesses, including their risk and protective factors—is better understood by the community.[9] If a community understands their risk and protective factors, they can then own these and evaluate them from their perspective. One example of this is the Communities that Care Program (CTC), which is a systematic approach to reducing adolescent problem behaviors in communities. Using a variety of tools provided under CTC, communities can identify and measure their risk and protective factors, select prevention programs aimed at reducing risk factors and strengthening protective factors, and chart their progress. The goal of the CTC operating system is to help communities increase the likelihood that they will select and implement prevention programs that fit their risk-factor profiles (Hawkins et al., 2009).

Finally, regularly scheduled meetings between researchers and community members should be established to provide an open channel of communication. These meetings provide community stakeholders with an opportunity for consistent input on the collaborative effort. In a sense, their views and comments come to be "expected" at the table.

Choosing the Degree of Collaboration
Researchers should consider, at the outset, the degree of collaboration they envision. A framework to think about the different levels of collaboration is best visualized along this continuum:

communication → coordination → collaboration

In a true collaboration, the traditional research model designed to answer a vast array of academic questions, should be abandoned. A collaboratively designed study may not answer the range of academic questions, but hopefully, it will better serve the community as they affect the questions asked and solutions offered. The participation of a community in a research varies, and it includes communities as (McKay et al., 2004):

1. Advice or consent givers (hiring consultants to provide advice on the community under study—generally a one-way flow of information)
2. Gate keepers and endorsers of the research
3. Deliverers of research or programs (e.g., frontline staff)
4. Active participants in the direction and focus of the research as members of community advisory boards

Most collaborative research begins at the first level and moves toward the fourth level. This fourth level has been considered ideal for research and program delivery in underserved, low-income minority communities (McKay et al., 2004).

Finding a Home for the Collaboration

Finding a home for a collaborative research project is not easy. For young children and adolescents with mental health issues, multiple state and county agencies are often involved in their care. In general, researchers looking for a partner at the state level can find one in the various health and human services systems that meet children's mental health needs, including child and adolescent mental health departments, and health, foster care, and the juvenile justice systems.

Determining How to Best Package and Present an Intervention

Know your audience.   Learn who your audience is and how to package and present information to them. Parents, teachers, and providers know and understand their limits of participation; focus groups can help draw out this information. For instance, mental health providers will accept a very different treatment package than researchers and patients (e.g., a 36-session treatment program, even if deemed effective, is unlikely to be paid for by most managed-care or service delivery organizations, or even patients, with or without insurance). A threshold should be determined, early on, as to the acceptability of an intervention, and the subsequent packaging to providers or patients.

Choose syntax carefully when presenting the intervention to the community.   Finally, in presenting an intervention to the community, pay careful attention to word choice. Some words, particularly academic or medical terminology, come loaded with double meanings. In most cases, the word *research* means something different to parents (conjuring up the notion that their child will be a guinea pig if they participate in the intervention) than to researchers. Similarly, the word *diagnosis* should be used with great care, as it comes attached with many meanings.

Paying Careful Attention to Study Design Issues

There are many important methods/study design issues that may require thoughtful attention when conducting collaborative community research. Some of these include:

- Treatment fidelity and the competing need for flexibility and compromise
- Quality assurance
- Efficacy versus effectiveness
- Understanding who participates and why

Treatment fidelity and the competing need for flexibility and compromise. The "by-the-book" implementation of a planned intervention is a thorny issue in traditional research. Any "drift" in implementation can cause skewed results; however, how much drift is acceptable is not known. For the majority of treatments, the active ingredients or mechanisms of change have not yet been identified or are not well understood. Fidelity can be an even stickier issue in collaborative efforts because the compromise often required can alter outcomes. That the need for flexibility and compromise is great when collaborating cannot be understated.[6] Balancing the two can, however, be done by paying attention to the characteristics of the community and those who are employed to deliver the intervention to them. Indeed, the most difficult issue is whether researchers can integrate community needs with sound methodologies (see Case Study 5).

Quality assurance. How an intervention is delivered, as well as who delivers it, as discussed above, is critical to obtaining the wanted clinical outcomes. Transporting treatments from university-based settings to communities can be complicated, with no "in-clinic" close supervision. One example of the implementation of a comprehensive quality assurance (QA) program, simultaneously with the intervention, shows how the QA program improved fidelity to the model and ultimately child outcomes (Henggeler, Schoenwald, Liao, Letourneau, & Edwards, 2002; Schoenwald, Sheidow, & Letourneau, 2004; see Case Studies 6 and 15 for examples).

Efficacy versus effectiveness. One research conundrum is how to achieve efficacy and effectiveness at the same time. Often seen as competing paradigms, efficacy may be favored by the research community, and effectiveness by the practice community (Hoagwood et al., 2001; Stricker, 2000). Some are calling for researchers to abandon efficacy trials because they lack application in real-world settings, in the communities in which they are desperately needed. Hybrid studies, a combination of both efficacy and effectiveness principles, have been developed to address some of these criticisms (August et al., 2004; see Case Study 7).

Understanding who participates and why. In any research, understanding who participates and why matters; it impacts the generalizability of the findings and the usefulness of the results. Understanding who participates and why is key to planning for future trials, particularly the development of better methods of recruiting those who resist participation or are likely to drop out. The first step in establishing a partnership base for research is to understand the "no's" of the participant community (Fantuzzo, McWayne, & Bulotsky, 2003; see box below);

doing so requires abandoning planned research for awhile, but recognizing and respecting these views generates critical information, including common problems that the researcher and the community may share. The struggle is to engage those who do not participate—and to understand why (active vocal, unsuccessful participation). If researchers can genuinely engage with this portion of the community, they can influence the questions asked and ultimately influence how the intervention is constructed.

Determining Whether the Program Is Feasible

Before collaborations can even begin, researchers need to ask: Is it feasible that this program/treatment can be implemented or adopted? By the community? By the providers who pay? If it is not feasible or likely to be adopted, perhaps resources would be better spent on community prevention, education, or other treatment programs.

Making the Budget Transparent and Recognizing Fiscal Limitations

Federal funding of collaborative research projects has increased 300% in the last 12 years. Recently, The National Institute of Mental Health, in a report issued to guide research on children's mental health (NAMHC, 2001), expressed a desire to fund more collaborative community research. The report called for the research community to "partner with families, providers, and other mental health stakeholders and policymakers to realign current resources to ensure that the science base on treatments and services is usable, implementable, disseminated, and sustained in the communities where children live."

There are four important funding-related issues that researchers should address. The first and often most important is to make the budget transparent to the community. (See Case Study 2 for an example of the importance of making the budget transparent.) The second is recognizing the limitations of the funding source. Regardless of source of funding (federal, state, local, or private), researchers should be aware of the constraints placed on collaborative activities, as funders sometimes dictate how much "say" the community can have in the design and implementation of interventions. Third, do not overpromise; estimate conservatively what you can deliver within your given budget. Finally, consider alternate funding sources; oftentimes, foundations are more willing to fund the "start-up" period, the year spent defining the community and designing the study, that community collaborations often require.

Building in Sustainability Up Front

Strong collaborative partnerships are crucial to ensuring that effective and innovative prevention and treatment programs can be sustained once research funding has ended. Sustainability is the ability of the community to maintain the treatment or intervention once the researcher has departed the community. In many cases, the sustainability of a program rests on whether the program has been successful in the community, which often rests on the availability of data. A community's ability to sustain a program also depends on whether community members were intricately involved in the design and deployment of the program (e.g., either as members of collaborative boards or staff members). Finally, training and technical assistance are key to sustaining programs in the community (see Case Study 8 and Case Studies 19–22).

CASE STUDIES OF COLLABORATION ISSUES

Each collaborative project presents its own unique challenges. The issues outlined in the case studies below may not arise in every collaborative effort. Different types of programs and interventions, as well as community history, dictate potential problem areas.

The Basics of Collaboration. Case studies 1–8 are related to the basics of starting and maintaining a collaborative project, including issues related to methods and design (contamination, fidelity, quality assurance, and efficacy vs. effectiveness) and sustainability.

Context and Culture. Case studies 9–13 address the issues of understanding the context and culture of the collaborating community, and developing interventions to fit the community's needs.

Setting-Specific Issues. Case studies 14–18 provide examples of issues related to specific collaborative settings, including schools, community-based care (e.g., home, clinic, and foster care), primary care/pediatric practice, and Head Start settings.

Evaluation and Sustainability. Case studies 19–22 illustrate the issues related to evaluating and sustaining collaborative endeavors, including the importance of data collection and evaluation, the use of collaborative boards, and the provision of training and technical assistance to sustain programs in the community. Case studies #23 and 24 illustrate steps involved in launching experimental studies that examine processes of collaboration among family advocates, providers and services researchers.

SECTION I. THE BASICS OF COLLABORATION (CASE STUDIES 1–8)

CASE STUDY 1

Building Trust and the Complex Issue of Using Money as an Incentive

The Early Risers Program

Gerald August and George M. Realmuto

The University of Minnesota, Center for Prevention and Children's Mental Health, Pillsbury United Communities, and Minneapolis Public Schools

The Early Risers Program for "at-risk" children offers an example of the difficulties of building trust within a community where parents may be leery of "helping hands." The Early Risers program, a violence and drug prevention program implemented in inner-city, predominantly African American and rural/semi-rural areas, provides comprehensive services for children and families via home visits and at centers or schools. The program is guided by a collaborative partnership forged among three major community sectors serving the metropolitan Minneapolis area: program developers at the University of Minnesota (Dr. Gerald August and Dr. George Realmuto), Pillsbury United Communities, and Minneapolis Public Schools.

One of the most difficult issues the researchers encountered was the community's perception that poor African American youth would be exploited in the course of the research. To address this issue of exploitation head on, the Collaborative assembled a cultural competence advisory board, which included a culturally diverse group of prominent community opinion leaders, educators, health-care professionals, and parents. Each member possessed an insider's understanding of the indigenous structure of the African American community and knew the most effective ways of making contact with, and gaining the trust of, community residents. The goal of the cultural competence advisory board was to create bridging relationships to connect poor, culturally diverse families with community agencies, and to bring together a coalition of resources to prevent violence in the community. To optimize its role in building community trust, the board was empowered to offer modifications to the program that would facilitate their acceptance by consumers in the community. Many of these modifications were adopted, and they included such adaptations as teaching the social skills curriculum through the presentation of African American songs, stories, and legends; facilitating literacy acquisition with reading materials that featured African American folklore; and incorporating the extended family system (e.g., aunts, uncles, grandparents) in parenting skills education and family support.

Solution
Researchers gained the trust of the community and countered their perception of exploitation by spending enormous amounts of time with them to build trust and to talk about their mutual interests. Emphasis was placed on the political and conceptual interest in helping the community and in getting people connected to available services within the community. In this instance, the local community center, Pillsbury United Communities, was used as an intermediary to make a connection to the community.

Key Point
While the collaboration was very difficult initially, trust was built once shared interests were clearly spelled out. "Building trust" is not a phase that can be passed through—it is ongoing. Much work will be needed along the way to maintain that trust.

The Intertwined Issues of Money and Trust

Money, in both traditional and collaborative research projects, is another complex and often complicating issue (i.e., there is rarely enough). In many traditional research and community-based collaborations, money can also present an ethical quandary. While important issues range from who is in control of the money, to how the money is spent, even more difficult is the combined issue of *ethics and money*, and the resulting perceptions (and misperceptions and mistrust) that money can create.

The Early Risers Program, the violence and drug prevention program discussed above, reveals how difficult the issue of payment for participation in a research endeavor can be. The recruitment of African American children from the inner city was challenging in and of itself, due primarily to issues of mobility of the families. The issue of payment to parents for participation in the prevention initiative raised difficult issues. Some in the community were offended by the idea that researchers would "pay" parents to participate in parenting education and take a more proactive role in their child's health and academic development. Payment for participation can often be culturally loaded, and in this case, many in the African American community interpreted the payment as further exploitation, asking the question, "Do we have to pay parents to be good parents?"

Solution

To resolve this issue, a discretionary fund was created for parents that would allow them to use the money to pay for child-care and/or transportation costs to facilitate participation in program activities, as well to assist in the purchase of basic living materials (e.g., rent, food, and clothing) and family activities. In this case, money was an important incentive, and once reframed, was viewed differently by program providers, as well as others in the community and even some parents. The lesson learned here is that money can be an extremely powerful incentive to raise family enthusiasm for participation in health promotion programs. When money is viewed ASA way to "bribe" families into participation, the wrong message is given. When dispensed in creative ways, it can enhance a program's impact without conveying a condescending tone. For example, one successful method employed by Pillsbury United Communities to sustain poor, African American families in health promotion activities is the FANS program. The FANS program engages youth in competence-building activities and commits funds for college scholarships to any youth who graduates high school in good standing and maintains a drug- and crime-free lifestyle. To date, the FANS program has graduated 49 youth, who have earned $180,750 in scholarships.

Key Point

Money issues will sabotage a project if not appropriately and sensitively addressed at the outset of the collaboration. In this case, the issue was reframed and presented to the community in the form of services that participants would receive for participating in the program.

CASE STUDY 2

Building Trust and Being Transparent about the Budget

The Collaborative HIV Prevention and Adolescent Mental Health Project (CHAMP)

Mary McKay

Mt. Sinai School of Medicine, The CHAMP Collaborative Board

The Collaborative HIV Prevention and Adolescent Mental Health Project (CHAMP) is a prevention program aimed at reducing the risk of HIV among adolescents, particularly urban African American youths, one of the fastest growing populations at risk for HIV infection. The program aims to assist families in helping their adolescents reduce their time in sexual situations and to strengthen their decision-making and refusal skills (McKay et al., 2004). The CHAMP program, which was initially implemented in Chicago, is currently being replicated in New York City, as well as three other locales overseas. In each location, the driving force behind the CHAMP program has been the Collaborative Board established to both guide and sustain the program in each community (i.e., The CHAMP Collaborative Board). The Board is a formal partnership between representatives of inner-city communities and the university researchers, and it also includes parents, school staff, and representatives from community groups.

Complex yet different issues of money and trust were also raised in this program. The CHAMP program is partially funded by a federal grant from the National Institute of Mental Health. Under the terms of the grant, direct costs

---

Money and Trust

"In many cases, money is not the real issue ... the real issue is trust that the community has in the researchers. The community is not really sure that they want your help or your money.

And, you know as researchers that you are good people, and it's hard to understand the perspective that a community may have that they are 'doing fine without you.' Oppositely, it is often hard for communities to understand that researchers are here to help, because many researchers before have come and gone and left the community none the better. Many times this issue of trust gets played out in terms of the money issue."

Dr. Mary McKay, CHAMP principal investigator

were split equally between the university and the community, but the university receives a large percentage of the grant money (69%) for indirect costs (overhead). This was a very contentious point with the community, and the high rate of overhead was difficult for the community to understand.

Solution
In this case, researchers made available to the community board the entire budget of the CHAMP program, with the details clearly explained from the beginning. Researchers gave a detailed description of the federal grant process, including the mandated overhead that universities receive under federal grant laws. While the board members thought this was unfair, they all agreed not to like it, but were able to move past the issue once researchers explained the federal grant process.

Key Point
Fully disclosing and explaining budget information to the community at the outset of the collaboration can prevent misunderstandings about money, and even more importantly, can do much to prevent mistrust between the researchers and the community.

CASE STUDY 3

Identifying Shared Goals and Delivering Results in a Timely Fashion

Susan Essock

College of Physicians and Surgeons, Columbia University

Meeting children's mental health needs is the job of many different child-serving organizations in a community, including the state departments of health and human services, education and juvenile justice, as well as county-level agencies. Researchers have a variety of potential agencies with which to partner. The case study below illustrates some best practices in collaborating with state agencies.

As the Director of Psychological Services for the State of Connecticut's Department of Mental Health and Addiction Services, Dr. Susan Essock undertook a collaborative research effort with university-based researchers and Connecticut's three state hospitals to study the costs and effectiveness of using clozapine for severely mentally ill patients in the state's mental health system. The use of clozapine, which cost $8000 per year, per individual treated, presented a very expensive proposition for the state. At the outset of this collaborative endeavor, researchers conducted a pilot study, which determined that fewer state patients would qualify for clozapine use than initially calculated; the pilot study revealed that of the 803 patients with a diagnosis of schizophrenia, only 60% of them met the Federal Drug Administration guidelines for treatment with clozapine (lack of response to two adequate treatments or unacceptable side effects using current drug therapies). Results of the full study indicated that once discharged, clozapine patients were less likely to be readmitted to state hospitals (Essock, Hargreaves, Covell, & Goethe, 1996).

Now a researcher with a joint appointment at both a university and at a state agency, Dr. Essock suggests that when collaborating with state agencies, researchers:

- *Be humble and respect the knowledge of collaborators.* In this instance, the professionals running the state program knew what life was like "on the ground." Their practical knowledge of children's needs in their state is invaluable. When this practical knowledge is meshed with researchers' academic knowledge, there may be great synergy, and areas of overlapping knowledge and potential projects can be identified.
- *Be flexible and respectful of their time.* Treat the potential collaborator's time as if it is more valuable than yours. If you want to work with the administrators of state programs, you need to go to them.
- *Deliver results within a time frame that is useful to administrators.* For instance, while researchers may want to implement a randomized clinical trial over a 3-year period, current mental health commissioners may not find this very useful, as they may be gone in 3 years.
- *Know the lay of the land—what is the collaborator's biggest problem?* Understand the issues that the agency is facing and offer to conduct analyses to help them decide how to allocate scarce resources. For instance, though providing an analysis of epidemiological data is a simple task for researchers, it is highly valued by state employees (often pressed for time) because it will help them to better understand their population and allocate scarce resources.

Key Point

When working with collaborators, including state agencies, researchers should take the time to learn *their* most pressing issues and plan to deliver results within a time frame useful to them.

CASE STUDY 4

Working with Collaborators to Interpret Findings

Patricia Moritz

National Center for Children, Families, and Communities, University of Colorado School of Nursing

David Olds

Nurse–Family Partnership National Science Office, Denver, Colorado

Peggy Hill

Nurse–Family Partnership National Science Office, Denver, Colorado

The collection, analysis, and interpretation of study data demand a slightly different process when done collaboratively. One example of this is the implementation of the Nurse–Family Partnership program, a prevention effort aimed at improving the health and well-being of at-risk children and their families (Olds, Hill, O'Brien, Racine, & Moritz, 2003). During a home visitation, nurses help mothers and other family members improve their health behaviors, the care of their children, and encourage personal development. The program began as a randomized trial in three locations (Tennessee, New York, and Denver) and is now deployed in 22 states.

In the course of implementing this prevention program in a Midwestern state health department, the researchers and state agency employees conducted their own separate analyses of evaluation data of the program and arrived at different results, which caused some concern among the group. After discussions and fact finding, we found that if the same variables, time frame, and analytic methods were not used, the results were different. In this case, the principal issue was different time frames and changes in data details. Credibility was established by all parties once the issue was clarified.

Solution

The researchers discussed in extensive detail how the data collection and analyses were conducted. In the course of this meeting, the researchers discovered that miscommunication caused the concerns about the evaluation results, with the state analysis based on a different time frame and analytic approach. Researchers clearly outlined the methods they were using and delineated the time frame on which data were based, and the issue was resolved.

Key Point

Extensive training, particularly in the data collection methods being used for the study, and clear, regular communication (e.g., at least monthly meetings) are required across the continuum of data collection, analysis, and interpretation to prevent difficulty in the evaluation and publication of results.

DATA DRIVE THE POTENTIAL FOR SECURING FUNDS TO MAINTAIN A COLLABORATION

Bill Hildenbrand

Executive Director, Savio House

While evaluating the outcomes of community collaborations can be difficult, data on outcomes are important, particularly to community funders. Savio House, a community-based mental health organization located in Denver, Colorado, is one

The Blueprints Project

The Blueprints for Violence Prevention program has identified 11 prevention and intervention programs that meet a strict scientific standard of program effectiveness. Program effectiveness is based upon an initial review by the Center for Study and Prevention of Violence, and a final review and recommendation from a distinguished Advisory Board. The 11 model programs, called Blueprints, have been effective in reducing adolescent violent crime, aggression, delinquency, and substance abuse. Another 19 programs have been identified as promising programs. To date, more than 800 programs have been reviewed, and the Center continues to look for programs that meet the selection criteria.

Source: http://www.colorado.edu/cspv/blueprints/index.html

example of how research data can drive the potential for getting funds to maintain a project. Savio House provides a variety of services to Denver youth, including residential and day treatment programs, foster placement, and many education and counseling programs.

Late in 1998, Savio House was selected as a multisystemic therapy (MST) implementation site as a part of the Blueprints program, a collaborative effort between federal, state, and local governments in Colorado to identify evidence-based violence prevention programs and test them in sites around the country. Savio House had used a home-based treatment program for many years, so when they considered MST, the program was a "good fit" with the agency's mission and goals; existing home-based services had improved outcomes, and the addition of MST would further improve adolescent outcomes. In Savio's application for the Blueprints program, they indicated that data collection was an important component of the program, and they worked to improve existing efforts. This focus on data collection, and wanting to be a leading edge agency with effective outcomes, assisted in the selection of Savio House as a Blueprints site.

Since Savio began implementing the MST program in 1998, demographic/process and outcomes data have been collected. Demographic/process data collected include age upon admission, ethnicity, adjudications, and length of stay, as well as therapist adherence measures. Outcome data include information on whether the adolescent committed any offenses during treatment, remained in his/her home (prevention of out-of-home placement), transitioned to a public school, as well as the percentage of treatment goals achieved. All data are collected by an administrative coordinator, when the budget allows; with recent cutbacks, this responsibility is now shared by clinicians and supervisors. The ability to produce outcome data on the effectiveness of MST has meant the difference in whether the program continues. Most purchasers of Savio House are accustomed to getting good outcomes for their referrals. One county government, during a period of reduced funding, noted that they were dropping all in-home services but would fund Savio House because data indicated children receiving MST there had positive outcomes. Perhaps as a sign of times to come, the State of Colorado has gone as far as to earmark state funds for use only on evidence-based interventions.

Key Point

William S. Hildenbrand, the executive director of Savio House, explains:

> Data collection is critical to sustaining programs but also to steering the ship. I believe you can't really know where you are going if you don't know the outcomes of your services; this has been key to the success of this organization. Lastly and seldom mentioned, it is very important to know, for your own sense of personal value, if what you are doing is having a positive impact on the families you are serving. Life otherwise is like having your head in the sand.

CASE STUDY 5

Contamination and Fidelity

Mary McBride

Assistant Director, Clackamas County Mental Health, Clackamas County, Oregon

Special issues arise when conducting randomized clinical trials. An example is the implementation of parent–child interaction therapy (PCIT) in the Clackamas County mental health system, one of the federally funded system-of-care sites in Oregon. The goal of the trial, funded by ORC-Macro, is to evaluate the effectiveness of PCIT for families receiving care within a system-of-care community, such as the one in Clackamas County. The families served are those who have children with severe emotional disturbances and are eligible for publicly funded mental health services. Many of these live within the "culture of poverty" and are involved with multiple community agencies.

The study is a randomized clinical trial, whereby half of the families receive PCIT in addition to the treatment they receive in the system of care, and the other half receive treatment as usual available within the system of care. A parent/child-focused treatment, PCIT is short term but intensive. Treatment families were initially asked to commit to a weekly 2-hour treatment session. Treatment clinicians had to maintain flexibility with service planning when implementing PCIT. Just like with any group clinical intervention, some families needed to do some individual or focused work prior to starting PCIT. There were times when PCIT had to be interrupted and suspended for a while due to crisis issues. Researchers explained to the control group that they were not receiving the PCIT, but, if results at the end provided positive, they too would be able to receive PCIT at the end of the

"Conducting a randomized clinical trial in a publicly funded community mental health agency brings many challenges to traditional researchers. Our agency experienced organizational changes due to budget reductions that included office moves, staff turnover, administrative shuffles, and service delivery model changes. Despite these, the study continued. These changes are part of the real work of publicly funded mental health and are variables that need to be identified and defined. They are not signs of failure or reasons to stop implementing evidence-based practices or evaluating their effectiveness."

Mary McBride

study. Parents in the control group did not perceive that they were not receiving treatment (since they received treatment as usual). Some parents perceived the promise of PCIT at a later date, if needed, as a positive motivator.

Fidelity

Fidelity to the model is one difficult problem that arises in randomized controlled clinical trials. "Good" clinicians are those who have educated themselves, been certified in various methods; all of their education and experience "morphs" into how they manage their clients day to day. They amass a "whole bag of tricks" and rely on these during therapy sessions with their clients. This morphing is a complex problem in the implementation of research studies, as clinicians are expected to follow a standardized treatment manual. In order to maintain fidelity to the treatment model, the study coordinator and PCIT expert consultant have a monthly teleconference to review the treatment manual and study goals and to problem solve issues. While there are checklists that help therapists adhere to the treatment manuals, there must be a bigger force to maintain fidelity—clinical supervisors must really delve not just into whether the checklists are completed, but review *how* therapists are doing the treatment. Clinical supervisors need to spend time observing as well as listening to the treatment clinicians discuss the PCIT work they are doing.

Contamination

The issue of contamination is one that in this instance is made more difficult by the co-location of the treatment and control groups. Due to severe budget cuts, two locations were combined to save staff and treatment dollars. While the co-location of the control and treatment groups made no difference to the families, it did impact staff. It was difficult for clinical staff not to talk freely among themselves. The clinical supervisor had to create a way to allow this exchange to continue for everything but PCIT. Staff was regularly reminded that maintaining fidelity was essential to having confidence in the findings generated. Part of the monitoring of fidelity included making sure that there was not some "borrowing" of aspects of PCIT by control clinicians. Sometimes control therapists had to say, "You can't really talk to me about that."

In closely listening to the clinicians, two key issues emerged during the collaboration: *(a)* clinicians were forgetting that PCIT was not yet an evidence-based practice for the study's target population and *(b)* clinicians were committed and struggling to "make it work."

Key Point

There were several keys to making this collaboration work. The motivation of the PCIT-trained clinicians happened through the successes and challenges they experienced with their families using PCIT. For the control therapists, the rewards had to be intrinsic, such as making the study successful or knowing at the end of the study they would receive the same intensive training in PCIT that all treatment group clinicians received. Clinicians not traditionally involved in research studies had many questions and concerns initially, especially about the methodologies. Oftentimes, such struggles were phrased in statements about "ethical" concerns that control clinicians were being asked to provide a "less adequate service" and treatment families receiving PCIT were getting "favorite" status. The issues of "favoritism" were related to their attempts to make sure that families participated fully. Questions arose that included, "Should I hold the more desirable appointment times for PCIT families?" "Should I be more lenient with PCIT families when they don't show, come late or cancel a lot?" Discussing the issues and the rationale allowed clinicians to resolve their concerns.

CASE STUDY 6

Quality Assurance

Scott W. Henggeler

The Medical University of South Carolina

Transporting treatments from university-based settings to communities can be fraught with difficulty. One intervention where the issue of quality assurance has been tackled head on is the comprehensive quality assurance program implemented alongside multisystemic therapy (MST), a family-based mental health and substance abuse treatment program. The effectiveness of MST in treating serious antisocial behavior in adolescents has been demonstrated in 12 randomized trials (Henggeler, Schoenwald, Borduin, Rowland, & Cunningham, 2009). As a result of its success, the high demand for MST services in communities (licensed MST programs are operating in 11 nations and more than 30 states, treating 17,000 youth and families annually) required that the MST developers create a training and quality assurance package to insure that communities would, with fidelity to the model, achieve successful outcomes.

Solution

Developers of MST created a comprehensive training and quality assurance package to aid communities in the development and implementation of MST programs in communities throughout the country. Essentially, the quality assurance program supports the therapists' and supervisors' capacity to implement MST effectively and to achieve desired youth and family outcomes.

Key components of the program include (Henggeler et.al., 2009)

- Ongoing organizational *consultation* to address agency and community barriers to program effectiveness
- An intensive *5-day orientation* to MST theory and clinical procedures for clinical staff
- *Quarterly booster sessions* for clinical staff
- A *treatment manual* that specifies MST clinical practices
- At least *weekly supervision of therapists* by an on-site clinical supervisor trained in the MST supervisory protocol
- *Weekly phone consultation* with the MST team by an MST expert who follows a specified consultation protocol aimed at promoting program fidelity
- *Periodic feedback* from clients via an Internet-based adherence questionnaire

Key Point

Research indicates that when therapists and supervisors adhered to the MST protocol, youth outcomes improved. Additionally, research has shown that the weekly consultation provided to MST treatment experts can increase fidelity to the model. Incorporating a comprehensive, multi-level quality assurance program into the implementation plan will increase the chances that successful clinical outcomes will be obtained.

CASE STUDY 7

Efficacy and Effectiveness

The Early Risers Program

Gerald August and Dr. George M. Realmuto

The University of Minnesota, Center for Prevention and Children's Mental Health, Pillsbury United Communities, Minneapolis Public Schools

The Early Risers program, the drug abuse and violence prevention program discussed in Case Study 1, is an excellent example of the ongoing efficacy versus effectiveness debate. Researchers relaunched this efficacy trial as a hybrid "efficacy-effectiveness study" (August et al., 2004). To transport this efficacy trial to the community, researchers first brought together key leaders of community service agencies and stakeholders who understood the serious consequences of adolescent drug abuse, and supported the idea of embedding effective prevention programs in the community. This collaborative partnership included the school system, a community center that served many poor, urban families, and the university. The researchers focused on developing a "hybrid" trial, which included both efficacy and effectiveness characteristics.

Efficacy characteristics included the following:

- Enrollment of early elementary school-aged children screened for aggressive/ disruptive behavior
- Random assignment of participants to program or assessment-only conditions
- Provision of specialized training, program manuals, and technical assistance to the practitioners
- Provision of coaching, supervision, and fidelity monitoring by the research team
- Two years of continuous intervention
- Annual outcome assessments conducted by trained technicians

Effectiveness characteristics included the following:

- Use of neighborhood centers rather than schools as the primary service venues
- Employment of agency staff rather than experienced professionals as practitioners
- Use of senior agency staff as consultants rather than securing external experts
- Permission for the community agency to make program adaptations (with approval from the collaborative) in response to perceived difficulties arising with the original protocol

Key Point

The most daunting problem encountered by program developers in transporting evidence-based programs to community practice settings was, and is, persuading community practitioners to deliver the program with fidelity. For a successful collaboration and to facilitate community buy-in, adaptations were made to the original protocol. To ensure that the program's effectiveness would not be adversely affected, permission adaptations were reviewed by the collaborative.

"Local providers have a unique organizational culture and their own theoretical orientation regarding intervention. Consequently, they may resist using content and procedures required by the validated model, such as manualized curricula, milieu interventions, quality assurance assessment, and evaluation tools. Failure to deliver a program as intended can dilute a program's effectiveness, ultimately 'poisoning the waters' in the community for future program adoption." G. August

CASE STUDY 8

Sustaining Collaborative Programs

The Collaborative HIV Prevention and Adolescent Mental Health Project (CHAMP)

Mary McKay

Mount Sinai School of Medicine,
The CHAMP Collaborative Board

One of the chief complaints of community collaborations is that once the funding period ends, communities are unable to maintain the prevention or treatment programs set up by researchers. This situation is often referred to as "research hit and run" and leaves behind the children and families who had come to rely on the availability of these programs in their community. Strong collaborative partnerships are crucial to ensuring that an effective and innovative prevention and treatment program can be sustained once research funding has ended (see McKay, Chapter Two, this volume). Researchers in the field are working to develop models of best practices for sustaining programs, and to develop guidelines to help researchers rethink this problem. Some of the major questions researchers are addressing about the sustainability of collaborative efforts include the following:

- *Defining sustainability.* What should this include? What are they? How are they measured?
- *Developing a conceptual model of sustainability.* Before or after protocol development?
- *Timing of the measurement of sustainability.* Before or after effectiveness is established?

As detailed in Case Study 2, The Collaborative HIV Prevention and Adolescent Mental Health Project (CHAMP) is a prevention program aimed at reducing the risk of HIV among adolescents. The board, which guides the collaborative effort, is organized into several subcommittees to conduct its work: Implementation, Welcome (to orient new Board members), Research, Grant Writing, Curriculum, Finance, and Leadership committees. Of these, the Grant Writing, Finance, and Leadership Committees all play a hand in sustaining the program in the community once the research is completed (McKay et al., 2007). Over time, through constitution of the collaborative board, the degree of collaboration around the design, delivery, and testing of the CHAMP Family Program has evolved into a truly collaborative relationship, reflected in the significant role key community members play in the direction, leadership, testing, and dissemination of the findings (Madison-Boyd et al., in press; Madison, McKay, Paikoff, & Bell, 2000; McKay et al., 2004). In Chicago, the original implementation site, the work of the collaborative board has helped to transfer CHAMP to a community agency.

Three key elements of the CHAMP program that have promoted the sustainability of the program in that community include (Madison-Boyd et al., in press):

1. *The "CHAMP" culture,* which focused on maintaining interpersonal relationships, a commitment to participatory processes, shared value for inclusion and real-world relevance, all of which resulted in a "family management leadership style."
2. *Training and mentoring community members to lead;* from day 1, the collaboration operated in a "training/mentoring" mode.
3. *The project director as a key player* in the transfer of CHAMP from the university to the community, responsible for the day-to-day tasks and oversight of the transfer of the program to the community.

Key Point

At the earliest stages of the collaboration, researchers should make it clear that the research will come to an end—and the community needs to plan to sustain the program. One way to do this is to make sure that collaborative boards are staffed with community members—not just university-based researchers—to ensure that the community truly guides the work, believes in the work, and has the training and know-how to sustain it once the research project is completed.

SECTION II. CONTEXT AND CULTURE (CASE STUDIES 9-13)

The Surgeon General's Report on Culture, Race, and Ethnicity (U.S. Department of Health and Human Services, 2001) outlined a set of priorities for improving the mental health of all people in the United States, including children. Priorities outlined included reducing stigma, building on the science base, improving public awareness of effective treatment, increasing the availability of mental health providers, ensuring that state-of-the-art treatments are available and accessible, and reducing financial barriers. Most importantly, the report emphasized tailoring treatments to age, gender, race, and culture. Clearly, all of these concepts have not yet become embedded in the science of children's mental health, as evidenced by the high levels of unmet need for children's mental health services in minority populations.

Ethical issues in the field of children's mental health also present some difficult and complex entanglements for researchers. Many ethical issues that arose in the early years of children's mental health research can be traced to the reliance on the traditional "medical model" used to develop interventions. As the field has evolved and moved away from the medical model (developed more to protect researchers than research subjects) and more toward collaborative research, new ethical, social, and political issues are arising. Ethics are made even more complex because different cultures have different values surrounding many of the key issues in children's mental health research: different beliefs about diagnoses (and perhaps labeling) and treatment of mental disorders, about the role of the child in the family, about protecting the child, and about money, confidentiality, and privacy. While ethics issues often create a quagmire for researchers, research in this field is important because much can be learned about how to treat and prevent severe mental illness in adulthood by studying these disorders during childhood (Hoagwood, Jensen, & Fisher, 1996).

The case studies below show how researchers are working more closely with some of the communities where mental health care is needed most, and how building interventions based on the cultures and contexts in which children and families live is creating better-tailored services and producing more positive outcomes for children and their families. The need to account for ethical, political, and social issues in designing interventions is also addressed in Case Study 11.

CASE STUDY 9

Understanding the Culture of the Collaborating Community

Patricia Moritz

National Center for Children, Families, and Communities, University of Colorado School of Nursing
David Olds
The Nurse–Family Partnership Program
Peggy Hill
Nurse–Family Partnership National Science Office, Denver, Colorado

True collaborations or partnerships with those in the community illustrate how culture can become ingrained in the research. In conducting collaborations, researchers are never sure who teaches whom what worldview. And in many cases, by the end, the language used by each partner changes, with participants adopting researcher's language, and vice versa. In some instances, researchers learn that some words do not exist or are not used in certain cultures. Some phrases are chosen to trivialize or silence problems.

Another case study that illustrates the importance of understanding culture is the deployment of a prenatal prevention program to improve the health of American Indian women and their unborn children, a home visiting and community health clinic program that predated the Nurse–Family Partnership (NFP) program (see Case Study 22 for more information on the NFP). In Oregon, three separate American Indian tribes historically were consolidated as one by the federal government; the researchers deployed a prevention intervention program, using American Indian nurses of a different tribe. The intervention was intended to change the behavior of pregnant women. In the early stages of the program, the researchers found that there was no effect and increasing attrition—none of the women were adhering to the program.

Solution

Focus groups with elders, program participants, and their families led researchers to realize that the approach they were using was not appropriate. In Western ideology, if you educate pregnant women on prenatal care, they will want to do right by the developing fetus. In these American Indian tribes, as in many other cultural groups, it is culturally inappropriate to talk about the fetus. In these cultures, the emphasis is on the pregnant woman, not on the developing fetus; therefore, women did not avail themselves of prenatal care, despite few barriers, economic and otherwise, to care. In most cases, women only sought care just weeks before labor.

Key Point

Culture and context are the foundation of any intervention. The process of developing a culturally appropriate intervention is a give-and-take process, in which researchers may have to modify their designs or instruments. In so doing, researchers may feel that they are "losing the science" a bit, but these adaptations ensure that the right questions are asked and that effective interventions are developed.

CASE STUDY 10

Understanding Culture and Context

The Start-on-Success Scholars Program (SOS)

Margaret Beale Spencer and Joseph Youngblood III

The University of Pennsylvania, The National Organization of Disability, The Philadelphia Public School System

The Start-on-Success Scholars Program (SOS) in Philadelphia, Pennsylvania, illustrates how important it is to consider culture and context when collaborating with communities. The Start-on-Success Scholars (SOS) Program is a school-to-work transition program aimed at improving employment and education outcomes for inner-city youth in 9th–12th grades with learning or emotional disabilities. Partners in this collaboration include the National Organization of Disability, The University of Pennsylvania, the Philadelphia Public School System, and students and their families. The program is funded through the school system, with job placements provided by the University of Pennsylvania.

The SOS program is an example of a collaborative effort that highlights the difficulties in accounting for culture at several different levels: race, school, and work culture. Truly understanding these various cultures and their contexts is critical to gaining community trust, buy-in, and hence honest participation by all partners in the program. The program was designed by the collaborators to be developmentally appropriate, culturally competent, and contextually relevant (for additional background on the development of the program, see Youngblood & Spencer, 2002).

Deploying the program in the both schools and work sites, with the assistance of teachers, job coaches, and work-site mentors, required a lot of honesty and candor on all of the collaborators parts on race, class, culture, and context. Each partner had a cumulative history of what led these students into special education classrooms, and in many cases, youths' behavior had been directly tied to academic expectations of them. Drs. Spencer and Youngblood and colleagues knew that in this case, they also had to change the context in which these children were being educated: they were going to school where students were labeled "not smart." Overcoming the issue of labeling was a tremendous challenge; everyone had to be trained in a new way of thinking, including the schools, teacher, parents, job coaches, and mentors.

In the design of the program, students and their parents were made real partners, who were empowered to co-design the program and its various components. According to Dr. Margaret Beale Spencer:

> Looking at the historical context of racial discrimination and "able-ism," particularly in light of the soft and often undetectable disabilities of the students from the students' perspectives, enabled the students to engage in a more thorough and genuine self-appraisal process. As a result, students were able to focus on their abilities by filtering the negative images and stigmas associated with their community (i.e., school and neighborhood) and their respective disabilities. At the same time, however, they were also encouraged to acknowledge and confront their academic and emotional challenges and to use the supports provided through SOS as a bridge.

Some of the other main challenges, in addition to labeling and retraining the staff in a new way of thinking, included overcoming the notion that a "one-size-fits-all" program would work, and the quantity versus quality debate.

Key Point

Understanding the community is vital. As Margaret Beale Spencer explains:

> Our own work suggests that a significant amount of confusion emanates from the fact that we use frameworks or perspectives which ignore the fact that people are engaged in human development tasks often undertaken under difficult conditions. Models employed by policy institutions are sometimes driven by points of view characterized by a priori assumptions of pathology, deviance and deficits (i.e.,

narrow "gap" thinking), not individuals' human development pursuits attempted under unacknowledged, inhumane, and multilevel ecological conditions. Culturally sensitive, context-linked, and normal human development perspectives must be considered and integrated for communities to truly benefit from collaborations.

Extended Background

To develop the SOS program, researchers relied on the identity-focused cultural-ecological (ICE) perspective and employed the Phenomenological Variant of Ecological Systems Theory (PVEST) in the design of the intervention (Youngblood & Spencer, 2002). This approach focuses on simultaneously accounting for many facets of an adolescent's environment, including *(1)* special risk factors, *(2)* the net effects of supports versus stressors, *(3)* the reactive coping strategies employed, and *(4)* the emergent identities manifested. For instance, SOS provides academic programming and career counseling, but it also requires that the students describe and build on their own identity (e.g., life events and lessons learned are explored with the students), one of the core components of the ICE perspective, in order to better develop and "fit" future career opportunities.

Some of the main challenges of the program are as follows:

- *The system-level assumption that "one size fits all" and that any support is "good enough."* This assumption was a difficult challenge to overcome. More often than not, researchers believe this assumption stems from the long history of insufficient supports and unaddressed values, beliefs, and stereotypes that generally guide decision making from the top. The researchers' approach was more "process oriented," getting input from students, families, teachers, and worksites to further fine tune the training required of everyone for enhancing the acquisition of positive youth outcomes.

- *Quantity versus quality debate.* One of the tensions among the partners was serving more kids versus serving fewer, better. One of the first major challenges was expanding SOS from a 1-year program for high school seniors to a multi-year program for underclassmen. This decision was based in part on findings from first-year data related to drastically improved student outcomes (e.g., attendance, grades, and workplace evaluations). These findings helped to ease the tension around the quality versus quantity debate, and ultimately, the evaluation guided the program's development and evolution. With good outcomes in hand, students and partners became ambassadors for the program.

- *Workforce training.* New ways of thinking about young people and helping young people be more effective in job situations were needed. PVEST was used as an intervention to assist "adults" in the workplace with identifying new ways of thinking about and supporting young people. From a collaboration perspective, this meant being very clear about the expectations, roles, and responsibilities of all of the partners. The design of the intervention included regularly scheduled workshops and seminars, as well as sustained and coordinated supervision of youth across program contexts. An often overlooked benefit of this model was the alignment of the content and curriculum between students' class work *and* their work responsibilities.

CASE STUDY 11

Assessing Ethical, Political, and Social Issues for Cultural Variations

M. Brinton Lykes

Chair, Counseling and Applied Development and Educational Psychology Department; and Association Director, Center for Human Rights and International Justice, Boston College

One researcher's work to understand the psychosocial impact of violence (e.g., war) on children and adolescents illustrates the importance of developing interventions deeply informed by the prevailing culture's political, cultural, and social beliefs. In 1987, in collaboration with Dr. Margarita Melville, Dr. Lykes undertook a research project in Guatemala and Mexico focused on understanding and responding to the effects of war on Mayan children and adolescents. These child survivors of war witnessed massacres, lost parents to death or disappearance, lived under constant military occupation, and most were situated in extreme poverty. After several years of working with community health promoters, child-care workers, and educators to more fully understand the impact of the ongoing war, Dr. Lykes and colleagues from Guatemala and Argentina developed The Creative Workshops for Children. The Workshops offered child-care workers and other adults in local communities a resource through which children were invited to use drawing, story telling, collage, and dramatization to express themselves, thereby communicating some of their experiences of war and their emotional responses to them. Thus, children had a temporary environment of relative security, that is, a time and space where they could re-establish ties with other children and develop ties with adults who would accompany them in the midst of ongoing war and repression. Participating in these workshops allowed children to both express themselves and create the capacity to see themselves as something other than victims of the dehumanizing and traumatizing reality of war (Lykes, 1994).

The Creative Workshops developed over a multiple-year process. The international action-research team worked with a local key informant who visited Mayan communities and collaborated in the documentation, through observations and in-depth interviews of traditional healers and leaders, parents, and children, how community members understood earlier and present experiences of terror and survival. They also documented local childrearing practices, beliefs about time and the afterlife, rituals for grieving loss and death, etc. Through these processes, cultural traditions (e.g., oral story telling and dramatization) and resources (e.g., nature, plants) were identified as critical in these contexts and as possible tools with which children could share their stories of terror and express their losses in The Creative Workshops. Over time and through praxis (that is, training work-shops with local health promoters and child-care workers and workshops with children and reflection on these experiences), this local knowledge, as well as resources from community and cultural psychology, were combined to create The Creative Workshops. It was often challenging to build consensus across differing cultural beliefs and professional backgrounds, demanding openness and patience of all involved.

Developing this intervention required, among other things:

- Local collaborators embedded in the community who are *recognized and trusted* by members of the community while being open to working with "outsiders" or "the other" team (the international research team).
- *The systematization of local knowledge and integration of diverse and sometimes divergent systems of knowing over time.* The Workshops emerged within an action-research process that developed over an 8-year period, and included an iterative and interactive process of action and reflection with an interdisciplinary, international team of professionals, local health promoters, child-care workers, and children.
- *The capacity to manage complex and evolving relationships over time and across multiple cultural, linguistic, social, and professional communities.*
- The availability of *money.* Although critical to the project's success, funding was also problematic. For example, outside professionals were salaried, yet many rural community leaders were voluntary, operating within a different set of local reciprocal relationships. Developing trust required transparency, whereas discrepancies in pay, living expenses, and lifestyles, etc. challenged the team repeatedly.

Key Point

There are several key points or issues to consider. The first is the issue of *categorization.* "Outsiders" and "insiders" see each other in ways that may not accurately reflect either their own self-understandings or their social realities. This work required a persistent and flexible renegotiation of social identities. The second is the issue of *defining the community.* The definition of community shifts with context (e.g., relative to religion, political party, interests) and is situational, relational, and dynamic. Finally, consideration should be given to both *language and voice.* Some words do not exist in another language, making translation and interpretation exceptionally challenging. Moreover, local expressions, for example, Guatemalans talked about "*la violencia*" as opposed to the war, have developed for complex reasons—to minimize the impact of the war, and perhaps silence discussions—that often confuse outsiders or defy their logic. Finally, understanding and language evolve throughout the collaborative process, with local participants and outside researchers adopting each other's languages and creating a "third voice."

As Dr. M. Brinton Lykes explains, "As researchers we have to continually rene-gotiate our understanding of ourselves and of participant groups, insuring that ethical, political, and cultural considerations are actively and dynamically incor-porated into the processes through which we engage with local players to develop collaborative interventions."

CASE STUDY 12

Adapting Research to Context and Culture

The GANA Program: Guiando a Ninos Activos
(Guiding Active Children)

Kristen M. McCabe[a,c], May Yeh[a,c,d], Ann F. Garland[a,c], Anna S. Lau[e], and Gloria Chavez[f]

Three San Diego Mental Health Clinics
[a] *Child and Adolescent Services Research Center, Children's Hospital, San Diego*
[b] *Department of Psychology, University of San Diego*
[c] *Department of Psychiatry, University of California, San Diego*
[d] *Department of Psychology, San Diego State University*
[e] *Department of Psychology, University of California, Los Angeles*
[f] *School of Social Work, San Diego State University*

Although effective treatments and therapies have been developed for many child and adolescent mental health disorders over the last 25 years, little research has been conducted on treatments for ethnic minority children. For example, Latino children, who make up the largest ethnic minority group in the United States, are much less likely to receive mental health services than Caucasians, though their needs are as great or greater (Kataoka, Zhang, & Wells, 2002; Sturm, Ringel, & Andreyeva, 2003). Dr. McCabe and colleagues (listed above) have developed the GANA program, *Guiando a Ninos Activos*, or Guiding Active Children, specifi-cally for Mexican American children with behavior disorders. The GANA pro-gram is an adaptation of Parent–Child Interaction Therapy (PCIT), an efficacious intervention for young children with behavior disorders (Eisenstadt, Eyberg, McNeil, Newcomb, & Funderburk, 1993; Eyberg, Boggs, & Algina, 1995).

Researchers adapted PCIT using feedback from interviews conducted with Mexican American families and reviews of literature about Mexican Americans. Modifications were made to PCIT, and these were tested with therapists, experts, and families (for more information about the process, see McCabe, Yeh, Garland, Lau, & Chavez, 2005).

Key components of the adaptation of PCIT related to culture and context included the following:

- *Building trust.* The researchers are all members of the Child and Adolescent Services Research Center (CASRC), a National Institute of Mental Health–funded center that has a long history of developing collaborative relationships with community agencies, including those from child welfare, mental health, alcohol and drug services, juvenile justice, and schools. Thus, CASRC's substantial track record of conducting research responsive to the needs of community agencies and working with ethnic-specific agencies provided a solid foundation on which to further build trust. The CASRC also strengthened relationships with community agencies by providing data management and analysis to them so they could better understand and serve their own clients. The CASRC's long-term, mutually beneficial relationship with these agencies greatly facilitated access to client populations, and they were able to help formulate and answer research questions. The CASRC also strengthened these community partnerships by sharing personnel with community agencies (e.g., funding partial salaries of agency employees, who served as liaisons between researchers and agencies) and including representatives from agencies in research networks. Finally, the CASRC is also affiliated with the Children's Hospital and Health Center, a well-respected pediatric facility within the local community, which perhaps allowed them to avoid some of the negative stereotypes sometimes associated with university-based researchers.

- *Establishing common ground.* In adapting PCIT, the researchers were able to build upon their reputations and expand existing relationships in the clinical community. Dr. McCabe involved the directors of the three local clinics (which serve the largest number of Latino clients in San Diego County) in the planning phase of the proposal. The goals of the project were very appealing to all of the collaborators: the main goal of the project was to find ways to reduce disparities in mental health services for Mexican American families, a goal shared by the community agencies. The project also promised to bring improved clinical services to the local clinical community and to provide additional training and program resources to the individual clinics. Dr. McCabe met personally with the clinical staff of each of the participating clinics in order to describe the study and get feedback on methods for recruiting clinicians and families.

- *Recruitment issues.* Clinicians on the multidisciplinary expert panel and participants in the focus groups were largely recruited via the relationships formed early on with clinicians and families at the clinics. Clinicians were paid a modest $50 consulting fee, were invited to attend a dinner where the PCIT model was presented, and feedback elicited, including potential adaptations. Families were recruited to participate in focus groups via announcements in waiting rooms, or directly by their clinician, who provided them with a form to sign (giving the researcher's permission to contact the family directly). This method of recruitment was only successful because of the high degree of contact that Dr. McCabe had with the clinicians prior to recruitment (clinicians were not compensated for assisting in the recruitment of focus group participants). Family members were invited to participate in a focus group based on language and location preference; locations were selected to be maximally convenient for the families, in community facilities (e.g., libraries, community centers), and dinner and babysitting were provided. Mothers were generally eager to participate, and they seemed to enjoy the sessions; fathers, however, were more difficult to recruit, and given high rates of refusal and no-shows among fathers, individual interviews were conducted to ensure that fathers' attitudes and beliefs about the treatment program were included.

Some important lessons learned in the adaptation of PCIT for Mexican American families included (McCabe et al, in press): *(1)* conducting an initial assessment of the families to reveal beliefs at baseline; *(2)* reframing the intervention as education, not treatment (choosing language carefully); *(3)* conducting a comprehensive first-contact and leaving a good first impression (providing a lot of information, and really engaging the family in the program from the outset); *(4)* focusing on interpersonal relationships; expending great efforts on building rapport with families; *(5)* the importance of getting feedback from the parents, since focus groups revealed that the parents were unlikely to challenge authority; and *(6)* revising written materials to ensure cultural accuracy (in the translation and simplification of materials)

Other challenges not directly related to culture or context but relevant to the program's functioning included the *limits of the funding* (e.g., few dollars left for training and research assistants) and the fact that clinics were severely under-resourced (e.g., space and personnel limitations). Another challenge included the *shortage of Spanish-speaking providers* in the community; within any given clinic, random assignment to three different conditions was very difficult (because you need to have three Spanish-speaking clinicians all in the same clinic willing to see the clients). Finally, *insurance issues* posed a problem; different clinics accept different providers, posing a difficulty in the use of random assignment to clinics. These challenges led to some modifications to the program. Currently, student therapists are being used to avoid the insurance issue; student therapists do not get reimbursed, so the clinic can take clients with any (or no) insurance coverage. Finally, the research is conducted out of one clinic only, which is located in a largely Latino community and had PCIT rooms already available at the time of the study launch.

Key Point
Cultural adaptations of effective programs can be accomplished. One key in the development of the GANA program was the fact that is was not created as one-size-fits-all Mexican-American families. Even *within* the culture, differences in parenting/discipline were clear from family to family. A central component of the program was the baseline assessment of a family's beliefs on parenting/

discipline. Even during the course of the treatment, therapists assessed family beliefs, as they may change during treatment. Ongoing research is underway.

CASE STUDY 13

Adapting Measures to Culture and Context

Douglas K. Novins

National Center for American Indian and Alaska Native Mental Health Research, University of Colorado Health Sciences Center
And other researchers/evaluators, including James Allen, PhD, Gary Bess, PhD, Kenneth M. Coll, PhD, Pamela B. Deters, PhD, Christine Duclos, PhD, Brenda Freeman, PhD, Ethleen Iron Cloud-Two Dogs, MS, Pamela Jumper Thurman, PhD, Michele King, Pamela L. LeMaster, PhD, Gerald Mohatt, PhD, Mary Phillips, BA, Barbara Plested, PhD, Teisha M. Simmons, BA, and Linda Son Stone

The Circles of Care Programs (1998-2001) include the following:

- Cheyenne River Sioux Tribe, Eagle Butte, South Dakota— *Restoring the Balance Project*
- Choctaw Nation of Oklahoma, Talihina, Oklahoma—*Chi Hullo Li/Choctaw Nation C.A.R.E.S for Families*
- Fairbanks Native Association/Tanana Chiefs Conference, Fairbanks, Alaska
- Feather River Tribal Health, Oroville, California
- First Nations Community HealthSource, Albuquerque, New Mexico
- In-Care Network, Billings, Montana—*Circles of Care/A Shared Vision Project*
- Inter-Tribal Council of Michigan, Sault Ste. Marie, Michigan—*Nbwakawn Circles of Care*
- Oglala Lakota Tribe, Porcupine, South Dakota—*Wakanyeja Wape Tokeca*
- Urban Indian Health Board/Native American Health Center, Oakland, California

The federally funded Circles of Care Initiative, underway since 1998, is an example of attempts to meet the needs of more of children in the American Indian and Alaska Native communities. This program grew out of the recognition of the high prevalence of mental health problems among American Indian and Alaska Native (AI/AN) children and adolescents, the inadequacy of existing services for these children, adolescents, and their families, and the need for community-based strategic planning to improve these services. Grants are provided to these communities to develop initial health service programs for children with serious emotional disturbances (SED). Thus, Circles of Care is distinct from many research projects described in this casebook as communities themselves are funded to do this work and hire their own evaluators/researchers to assist them; as such, in this case study, the term *evaluators* is used. This model also includes the provision of technical assistance from university-based researchers to the communities, their program staff, and their evaluators/researchers.

One of the components of the Circles of Care evaluation process is to have grantees develop locally relevant definitions of serious emotional disturbance (SED). Grantees are able to define what SED meant in their community and eventual eligibility for services under their plans. The university-based researchers who serve as technical assistance providers encourage the grantees to consider development of a local definition of SED as initial discussions of this terminology at program-wide grantee meetings showed that many community members perceived the term "SED" as stigmatizing, and that some communities wanted to develop a more strength-based definition of SED. Furthermore, it was clear from these discussions that the DSM-IV diagnoses that form the foundation of the federal definition of SED were not likely to match up with local definitions of health and illness (Simmons, Novins, & Allen, 2004).

Most grantees evaluated the existing definitions in their community, discovering that many existed. These definitions are compiled by research and program staff, evaluated, and in some cases, sent to each grantee's advisory board (which includes parents, youths, elders, treatment providers, and sometimes elected officials). Some grantees developed new definitions of SED by working with an advisory board, focus groups, or Gatherings of Native Americans. Seven of the nine grantees who participated in the first cycle of Circles of Care developed their own definitions of SED.

Two key issues arose during this planning phase of the collaboration: trust and ethics (Novins, LeMaster, Thurman, & Plested, 2004). The review and potential redefinition of SED needed to occur during the first year of the project. This was problematic in that there was not sufficient time to establish trust or rapport between the evaluators, program staff, and community members. Indeed, communities were being asked to be forthcoming about particularly sensitive information without really knowing the evaluators. The second issue was that of ethics; communities were being asked for their input and support for a system that was as yet unfunded. For many, it was difficult for them to put hard work into the planning phase when they knew its eventual implementation was unclear. Ultimately, the frank and open discussion of these issues became an important part of the process for developing a strong, collaborative relationship between the evaluators, the project staff, and community members, a process which the Circles of Care participants have called an "evaluation lifecycle" (Bess, Allen, & Deters, 2004).

Key Point

"The analysis of existing definitions of SED and the new definitions that six of the grantees developed are among the most important products of the CoC initiative. What may be less clear, but is perhaps of more lasting importance, is the transforming nature that these exercises had on the grantee staff, their community partners, and the planning effort as a whole. The opportunity to discuss, analyze, and reconstruct the concept of SED was, for many grantee communities, an extraordinary exercise in empowerment and self-determination. In the end, rather than being governed by externally imposed, existing definitions, the grantees gained control of these definitions themselves. "Through this process, CoC communities became further empowered to envision how culturally appropriate services for AI/AN children and their families in their local communities might look, and further determined to make them a reality" (Simmons, Novins, & Allen, 2004, p. 64).

SECTION III. SETTING-SPECIFIC ISSUES (CASE STUDIES 14-18)

As discussed in the case studies above, both culture and context should drive decisions about research design, methods, and goals. Specific settings also dictate the adaptation of research methods and goals. The following case studies of research conducted in schools, communities (home, clinic, and foster care settings), primary health care, or Head Start settings provide examples of issues that research should identify and understand before collaboration begins.

CASE STUDY 14

School-Based Mental Health

Robert Campbell
The Department of Education, Director, Program Support and Development
Christina Donkervoet
The State of Hawaii, Department of Health, Chief, Child and Adolescent Mental Health Division
Bruce Chorpita
The University of Hawaii, Associate Professor, Clinical Psychology

In some communities, the school system provides one of the main avenues for early intervention or treatment for many children with mental health needs (Burns et al., 1995). As such, the school system presents an opportunity to reach many of the children in need of mental health services. In response to a 1993 legal decree that the state of Hawaii provide a statewide system of mental health care for its children and adolescents, the Departments of Health and Education, in collaboration with the University of Hawaii, undertook a major effort to identify evidence-based practices (EBPs) producing successful outcomes for children. The goal of this effort was to not only identify these best practices but to ensure that these were deployed in both the health and education systems serving children with mental health needs. As a result of this process, there has been a major reform of the way in which child and adolescent mental health services are provided in Hawaii's health and education systems, which serve approximately 10,000 children and adolescents.

In 2000, the first "evidence-based practices" were identified by an interagency committee and deployed in the school and health systems; the menu of EBPs was updated monthly after committee review. The committee then focused on the development of a database system to measure actual practice and outcomes (including information relevant to youths' individualized service plans). The database is used to compare practice and outcomes published in the literature to what each student is receiving, and identify missing elements in their service plan. This initiative affects the approximately 500 youth with the most severe mental disorders.

The Department of Health (DOH) and Department of Education (DOE) provided systemic leadership for this initiative, as well as funding. An interagency committee, The Evidence-Based Services Committee, composed of DOH and DOE employees, in partnership with the University of Hawaii, was charged with reviewing the literature and identifying the evidence-based practices "that work." After identifying these EBPs, the committee disseminated this information and provided training to both schools and state-based practitioners; the same clinical standards manual was used for both DOE and DOH.

One primary issue was the difficulty in trying to change both attitudes and practice. Researchers noted that while extensive training and technical assistance materials can be developed and deployed, the publication of these materials tends to do little for changing practice without someone to guide the process at the "ground level" to encourage their adoption. Dr. Chorpita served as the clinical services office director of the Child and Adolescent Mental Health Division of the Department of Health for 2 years, bringing the concept of evidence-based practice to all levels of the child-serving system. After 2 years, the process became routine, with employees consulting the "menu" of evidence-based practices identified. Another important component of this successful collaborative effort was monitoring structure that was developed and put in place to measure practice and outcomes—against practice and outcomes reported in the literature.

Parents approached the DOE and DOH with concerns about the availability of prevention programs for young children. In response, the joint DOH and DOE committee reviewed the literature on prevention programs for 3–5 year olds to identify prevention programs that work for preschool children. Finally, presenting information clearly and at the level that can be understood by parents, a key group of stakeholders, is critical, whether it be written or oral information. In this case, parents sometimes did not want the evidence-based practices that had been identified because it "limited their choices." The Department of Health con-tracted with a statewide family organization to develop fact sheets in parent-friendly language, so that parents could understand both how the interventions were identified, as well as the outcomes. Committee members were also called upon to detail to parents the process of how these EBPs were identified and to explain the changes in the service system.

Approximately one new evidence-based intervention was (and still is) identified at the monthly Evidence-Based Services (EBS) committee meeting. This informa-tion then flows down from the committee to DOH and DOE training coordina-tors. From there, it is disseminated to a behavioral health coordinator, training coordinator, and then district educational specialists.

Key Point

Having an "agent of change" and also the system to measure that change—the processes and outcomes—is essential in any collaboration. As Dr. Christina Donkervoet (Hawaii Department of Health) said, "The system leadership set the stage for this collaborative effort—and we were the 'change agents' for this to be able to occur."

CASE STUDY 15

Home-Based Care

Multisystemic Therapy

Cynthia Cupit Swenson
Associate Professor, Family Services Research Center, Department of Psychiatry and Behavioral Sciences, The Medical University of South Carolina
Scott W. Henggeler
Professor, Department of Psychiatry, The Medical University of South Carolina; and The Union Heights Neighborhood Council and Union Heights Community Center

As discussed in Case Study 6, multisystemic therapy (MST) is a family-based mental health treatment program effective for treating serious antisocial behavior in adolescents. The Neighborhood Solutions Project is illustrative of a collabora-tive community program providing home-based care. The project was a collabora-tion effort between the state of South Carolina (Healthy South Carolina Initiative), the Family Services Research Center (FSRC) at the Medical University of South Carolina, and the neighborhood of Union Heights in the city of North Charleston. The goal of the project: to empower an economically disadvantaged neighborhood to address violent criminal behavior, substance abuse, and antisocial behaviors of youth while keeping them in the neighborhood. At the outset of the project, the neighborhood leaders identified the top six problems of youth in their community: violent crimes, substance abuse, drug dealing, child prostitution, vandalism, and school expulsions. After meetings with neighborhood parents, youth, elders and ministers, school personnel, City government, judges, law enforcement officers, and business leaders, three key problems were determined to be the focus of interventions: youth criminal activity, substance abuse, and behavior problems placing them at risk for school expulsion.

The community embraced the use of MST because of its emphasis on treating youth in their natural environments (e.g., school, home, and neighborhood settings). Neighborhood leaders also embraced MST because they were given scientific evidence that MST worked in reducing the kinds of problems that they had identified and were gravely concerned about. Together with the neighborhood, the FSRC staff determined that youth with serious clinical problems (school or crime related) would receive home and community-based MST. Youth with serious substance abuse problems (i.e., cocaine or marijuana) would receive intensive MST, plus specific substance abuse treatment via a community reinforcement approach. In addition, together, the neighborhood residents and FSRC staff developed and implemented neighborhood-based prevention activities, which provided alternatives to drug and criminal activity, increased neighborhood and family cohesion, and improved academic skills (Randall, Swenson, & Henggeler, 1999). Researchers worked to include all of the stakeholders' perspectives into the program, including community leadership of Union Heights (the president of the Union Heights Neighborhood Council and the director of the Union Heights Community Center), the community's schools, churches, and business leaders, and The Charleston County and City of North Charleston officials, who pledged support of programs and equipment, as well as the North Charleston Police Department and juvenile justice leaders (including judges), who pledged to help Union Heights leaders and the clinical team when youth were involved in criminal activities.

Challenges in implementing the Neighborhood Solutions project included the difficulty in gaining community trust and recruiting volunteers. While the community had a strong desire to participate, the issue of exploitation and trust was a difficult one to overcome. In the history of the neighborhood, majority groups and other "outsiders" had come in to arrest, harm, or buy drugs, so the intent of the program staff was suspect to the residents. Getting children and families involved in activities and recruiting volunteers was initially difficult. An outreach method was used to increase involvement; active recruitment of and weekly "rounds" with volunteers became a routine, scheduled part of the program. Volunteers assisted with violence prevention activities that took place directly in the neighborhood.

Providing activities in the community was essential, as most people did not have transportation. Volunteers were also involved with academic, recreation, family cohesion, and health and wellness activities, according to their strengths and skills. As word of the success of the project spread, volunteers from outside the community got involved.

Key Point

In a neighborhood, clinical work is not likely to be successful if it comes before establishing a true collaborative relationship with the residents. The key step to engaging stakeholders in neighborhood-based work is to take adequate time to complete the groundwork needed to earn trust, making sure to follow the advice of the people. To work effectively in a culture different than one's own also requires opening oneself to being a student, regardless of college degree, listening, and following the advice of a cultural guide. A consistent show of respect for and trust in stakeholders and consumers is also a key factor in program success. People living in neighborhoods know their children best and can advise on what they need. Canned intervention programs from universities have less value than interventions developed with input from people in a youth's ecology.

Finally, providers of mental health services need to think and work "out of the box" for people who do not live a middle class "traditional" life. They need to be flexible and willing to work in nontraditional ways (e.g., holding a session in the street). Evidence-based practices can be delivered effectively if done so in ways that make sense to families in the community. Regardless of educational level or family income, most people want to know that services they are going to be involved in have some evidence of effectiveness. They deserve no less.

Extended Background

Many neighborhood residents were skeptical about trusting counselors, especially with regard to substance abuse treatment, as people feared that the intent was to have them arrested. Others worried that counseling implied they were mentally ill, or that they did not trust God to help with their problems. Regarding research, many adults in the neighborhood were familiar with the harm that occurred among participants in the Tuskegee study (i.e., economically disadvantaged black men were given syphilis and kept from a cure for the sake of research). Also, in the past, many researchers and program developers had used data from the neighborhood to gain grant funds, but they never implemented programs in the neighborhood. As a result, residents felt that something was taken from them, and nothing was given in return. The potential for harm to residents was a top concern. Because of the history of exploitation of this community and African American people, great care was taken by researchers and the FSRC staff to present this project not as something that the researchers would be doing to the community, but as something that they would be doing for themselves, with supportive resources. For instance:

1. FSRC researchers emphasized that residents would largely decide which problems of their youth would be addressed by the project.
2. FSRC carefully explained their philosophy of conducting interventions—that the family and systems are the primary vehicles used in the intervention
3. FSRC explained that they would act as facilitators or coaches of the intervention, similar to their efforts in other collaborations across the country.
4. FSRC showed the community leaders scientific evidence that the treatment approach had helped many youth and families—and was not an "experimental treatment being applied to guinea pigs."
5. FSRC researchers explained to the community that the research was to evaluate the work of the staff and to determine whether the interventions were helping. Residents were told about the Institutional Review Board (IRB) review process, the measures put in place to protect people who participate in research. The research plan was presented to the neighborhood residents and leaders at a community-wide meeting, and they voted to accept the research design.

Extensive training and technical assistance materials are available through MST Services, Inc. (http://www.mstservices.com). For the Neighborhood Solutions projects, researchers generally adhered to the standard MST model (clinical and quality assurance), on which research outcomes are based. The treatment was modified by adding a less-intensive clinical follow-up phase, and the Community Reinforcement Approach was adapted for treating cocaine use in the community. Working together, the community and MST team also developed, modified, and implemented violence prevention activities tailored to neighborhood needs, including procedures for working collaboratively with the police, the creation of a nursing team to provide health care, and procedures to sustain the violence prevention programs by making the neighborhood a nonprofit business. These procedures are outlined in detail in a collaborative book (Swenson, Henggeler, Taylor & Addison, 2005), written jointly by researchers and a MUSC nurse, community leaders, and three local police officers. For more information on training and technical assistance, see Swenson, Henggeler, Taylor, and Addison (2005) and Randall, Swenson, and Henggeler (1999).

CASE STUDY 16

Group and Foster Care–Based Care

Patricia Chamberlain

Oregon Social Learning Center, Center for Research to Practice,
The Oregon Youth Authority,
The Oregon County Juvenile Justice Systems

Research by Dr. Patricia Chamberlain testing the effectiveness of treatment foster care illustrates another type of community-based care. In this ongoing study, adolescent females (ages 12–16 years) recommended for placement in out-of-home care are randomly assigned, per an agreement with the researcher and local county judges, to multidimensional treatment foster care (MTFC) or group care (GC). In MTFC, girls are placed in foster homes where parents have been recruited and trained to provide treatment hypothesized to be related to good short- and long-term outcomes. Girls assigned to GC join 6 to 13 peers with similar delinquency problems. The goals of this study are to evaluate the outcomes of MTFC and GC girls, and to determine which components of MTFC contribute to short- and long-term outcomes, including antisocial behavior and delinquency.

Results on 12-month outcomes are available (Leve & Chamberlain, 2005), and analyses suggest that the MTFC program was more effective than the control condition in reducing the number of days the girls spent in locked settings ($p < .05$; a 62% greater reduction than in the control condition), and in reducing caregiver-reported delinquency ($p < .05$; a 35% greater reduction). In addition, the MTFC group showed a trend for a reduction in the number of criminal referrals ($p < .10$; MTFC girls had 42% fewer criminal referrals at follow-up).

Based on their history of chronic and severe juvenile offending, parole and probation officers in Oregon counties identify girls as needing out-of-home care, and contact study coordinators to enroll them in the study. Initially, the study sample was to be recruited from Lane County only, but fewer females (than males) were found with a need for out-of-home placement; therefore, the study was expanded to include those from all Oregon counties. In accordance with an agreement between the researcher and the Oregon Youth Authority, girls were then randomly assigned to placement in MTFC or GC. After the girls were referred, consent was obtained for their participation in the study (from the girl and her parent or guardian). Most parole and probation officers were very cooperative, with many pinning their hopes on having their client receive MTFC. Some who referred girls who had not received MTFC were hesitant to keep referring. However, the study recruiters worked to educate parole/probation officers to the benefits of families participating in the study itself and encouraged them not to focus solely on the outcome of the random assignment.

Key Point

It is a challenge to sell the idea that a flip of a coin determines whether a girl is accepted into the MTFC program. However, because the Oregon Youth Authority supports the research and researchers regularly promote the value of the study when talking to juvenile justice workers, there is usually a steady rate of referrals. Another challenge of the project is shifting priorities; for reasons beyond the control of the study, such as county budget cutbacks or agency restructuring, the pace of referrals can be altered, and not always for the worse. Maintaining contacts within the system helped researchers anticipate and prepare for such changes.

CASE STUDY 17

Primary Care/Pediatric Settings

Ardis Olson

Dartmouth Medical School; Clinicians Enhancing Child Health, a regional research network; Anthem Behavioral Health Network

Today, researchers estimate that up to three-quarters of children and adolescents with mental disorders receive no mental health care (Kataoka, Zhang, & Wells, 2002; Sturm, Ringel, & Andreyeva, 2003). More research is now being conducted on the role of primary care physicians and pediatricians in diagnosing and treating childhood mental disorders. The mission of one national network of pediatricians, The Pediatric Research in Office Settings Network (PROS), created in 1986 by the American Academy of Pediatrics (AAP), is to improve the health of children and enhance primary care practice by conducting national, collaborative practice-based research.

The PROS Network

As of January 2004, PROS consists of 1860 pediatric practitioners from 677 practices in 50 states, Puerto Rico, and Canada; a research staff at AAP headquarters; and research consultants from around the country (AAP, 2004).

The Pediatric Research in Office Settings Network undertook a large study to address the identification and management of attention-deficit/hyperactivity disorder (ADHD) in primary care (Wasserman et al., 1999) and the primary care treatment of pediatric psychosocial problems (Gardner et al., 2000). Data from this national network have impacted policy: data generated from this research (Wasserman et al., 1999) informed the new AAP guidelines for primary care physicians in diagnosing ADHD. While no one has yet done so, one application of this network would be to have researchers take results back to their community and design local interventions in light of the data collected. While PROS is an example of a national collaboration between pediatricians throughout the country and the AAP, regional research networks are conducting more "localized" research in their communities. Regional networks of primary care/pediatricians are located across the country; in and around Chicago, Illinois;

Columbus and Cincinnati, Ohio; Philadelphia and Pittsburgh, Pennsylvania; St. Louis, Missouri; Seattle, Washington; and Hanover, New Hamphire (http://www.aap.org/pros/netsum97.htm).

One example of collaboration with a regional network is the work of Dr. Ardis Olson and Dr. Allen Dietrich at The Dartmouth Medical School, funded by the U.S. Health Resources Administration (HRSA) and the Commonwealth Fund. Dr. Olson and Dr. Dietrich have been working with pediatricians statewide to improve the detection and treatment of depression in mothers with young children. Postpartum and maternal depression can have serious consequences for mothers and their children, including a mother's ability to attach to and parent her child. The researchers partnered with six community pediatric practices, all members of the regional pediatric research network Clinicians Enhancing Child Health (CECH). Created in 2000, CECH has 24 pediatric practices participating in a variety of research projects. The six pediatric practices, composed of nearly 30 doctors, agreed to participate in this project to develop a screening tool to identify mothers with maternal depression at well-child visits; those mothers identified with depression would then have available to them a toll-free support line for help.

Initial work to develop the screening tool vetted a paper screening tool against a scripted, verbal interview conducted by the pediatrician. Results of that test indicated that the paper screen resulted in identifying 22.9% of the women versus 5.7% for the verbal interview screen (Olson et al., 2005). This paper interview was tested on about 250 mothers attending well-child visits, was further refined to include a gauge of the severity of the depression, and retested with an additional 250 mothers. The finalized paper screener was then given to nearly 850 mothers. Today, approximately 9000 mothers have been screened. The second goal of the project was to provide a referral for treatment for depression. A large local insurance provider, Anthem, set up a toll-free support line that mothers could access.

Two issues emerged in the course of the collaboration. The first is that even in practices that understood the importance of the detection and treatment of maternal depression, it was hard to implement a change in practice. Researchers need to have champions on the ground, either in the nursing staff or administration, in order for their project to be successful, in this case, for their screening tool to be administered. The other important issue is that researchers have to both understand the demands that the pediatric practices face (or other setting, schools, community care, etc.) and also understand what is realistic for them to achieve working within that framework. In one case, the practice was just overwhelmed with getting day-to-day tasks done and could not administer the screening tool.

Key Point

Ardis Olson explains,

> Only by working hand-in-hand with your collaborators can you really understand what can be achieved in a "real-world" setting. For instance, we knew that

demographic data could not be collected due to time constraints; there are compromises that happen in data collection. The process of developing screening tools and an intervention has to be done carefully and within a realistic time frame.

CASE STUDY 18

Head Start

John Fantuzzo

The University of Pennsylvania,
The Department of Human Services, State of Pennsylvania, Participating Head Start Centers in Philadelphia, Pennsylvania

In 1990, Dr. Fantuzzo and colleagues began a partnership with Head Start centers and the Department of Human services in Philadelphia, Pennsylvania, to identify the risk factors for children's adjustment to school. The collaboration resulted in the eventual identification of child maltreatment as a significant risk factor for poor school adjustment, the subsequent development of new diagnostic measures, and an intervention to improve the school readiness of maltreated children (Fantuzzo, McWayne, & Bulotsky, 2003). Two major follow-on projects are also underway: the creation of better linkages between the Head Start program and the Department of Human Services, and the development of a collaborative, integrated, data sharing system among the school district, the Department of Human Services, and the Department of Public Health. For more details on this intervention and the findings from this study, see Fantuzzo et al. (2003); Fantuzzo, McWayne, and Childs (2006); Fantuzzo, Stevenson, Kabir, and Perry (in press); and Fantuzzo, Manz, Atkins, and Meyers (in press).

Understanding Community Resistance

Early on in the collaboration, study goals had to be reframed when the community strongly resisted the proposed research project. The researchers went back to the funder (The U.S. Department of Health and Human Services) and requested that the project timeline be extended so that additional time could be taken to better understand the "no's" in the community. For further information on the importance of understanding who participates and why, see the section in this chapter, "Key Principles of Collaboration" and Fantuzzo, McWayne, and Childs (in press).

At the outset of the collaboration, the majority of parental resistance was to the proposed use of the Child Behavior Checklist (CBCL), a widely used checklist of psychiatric symptoms associated with children's mental disorders. Initially, parents viewed the researchers as "privileged outsiders" coming into the communities to document their children's problems; teachers largely felt that the researchers were trying to diagnosis and label the children, giving no regard to the contexts in which they lived, learned, and played (Fantuzzo, McWayne, & Childs, in press). At the outset, researcher assistants set up tables outside Head Start classrooms to present the research process (including the measures to be used) and obtain informed consent for their participation. The majority of parents passed these tables by, upset about the measures used in the study, and whether this information would be shared with the government. Research assistants indicated that this information would be kept confidential, but parents were not satisfied. The general mistrust of the information presented caused the parent leadership to discourage others from participating in the project. Unwittingly, the research team erred by assuming that the agreement made with the Head Start administrators represented the concerns of the parents and teachers. This was not the case. Researchers then invited both parents and teachers to discuss their concerns about the use of CBCL, which they viewed as stereotypically focusing on the weaknesses and ignoring the strengths of children in their community. Lesson Learned: In the context of initiating research partnerships, it is essential to take *time and listen to all of the relevant community participants* before beginning your project.

As a result of these discussions, the Penn Interactive Peer Play Scale (PIPPS), a parent-measure of children's abilities, and the Adjustment Scales for Preschool Intervention (ASPI), a teacher-measure of children's social and emotional development, were developed. These two scales were developed with Head Start teachers, parents, and researchers as a better measure (than the CBCL) of children's ability to successfully engage in play with peers. But even more importantly, this dialogue led to broader discussions about attitudes toward research in the community, which were quite negative. Formal parent and teacher councils were set up to better understand parents and teachers considerable concerns about the research. The Head Start Policy Council met with the research team to review the research agenda, the measures to be used, and the goals and objectives of the research project. A special Research Committee of the Policy Council was established to work with the research team. This committee met monthly with the research team to receive updates on the research activities and talk with some of the parents working on the research team.

Because maltreated children were more likely to possess maladaptive peer play behaviors (than nonmaltreated children), researchers, in collaboration with Head Start teachers and parents, designed an intervention to improve the peer play of maltreated children. Teachers identified both those with difficulty engaging in positive peer play, and those who could serve as role models (or "play facilitators"). Parents were also selected to participate, based on their ability to interact with children in a supportive, child-centered manner. Training manuals were developed for the parents and teachers participating in the intervention. Also, manuals and professional development workshops were created to introduce the new measures that were generated as part of the collaborative research activities.

Key Point
Several key points emerged in the conduct of this collaboration. A substantial amount of time is required to establish a genuine community partnership and co-construct a research agenda. Researchers invested the first year of the project establishing a partnership base that was necessary to conduct a co-constructed research agenda. This appeared to put us a year behind our original agenda; however, the quality of the work produced in the partnership more than made up for the time delay. Moreover, the foundation created by this partnership served as the basis for over a decade of productive applied research to follow. It was only this genuine partnership that allowed the researchers to gain valuable information about culture and context. Second, cultivating the natural resources in the community was key to the development of an effective intervention. In this case, researchers employed the skills of those in the child's classroom and family context; researchers, along with Head Start teachers, identified and trained parents and socially skilled peers to carry out the intervention. According to Dr. John Fantuzzo, "Co-constructed interventions implemented in a natural classroom context and employing the skills of natural contributors can close the gap for child victims of maltreatment."

SECTION IV. EVALUATION AND SUSTAINABILITY (CASE STUDIES 19-24)

Do Collaborations with Communities Impact Child Mental Health Outcomes?

No studies to our knowledge have directly examined the differential impact of community collaborations on children's mental health. Are collaborative efforts improving children's mental health outcomes? In most instances, there is little time or money to spend on evaluation because community service needs are large (e.g., most children in need of mental health services do not receive them). That said, there have been limited efforts at evaluating collaborative community efforts, primarily because of the difficulty in evaluating these types of programs (Altman, 1986). Some work has been done evaluating the effectiveness of community coalitions, a recent review of the Communities That Care (CTC) programs indicates that these coalitions that focus on healthy youth development can impact their communities (Hawkins et al., 2009).

In 2000, the Centers for Disease Control and Prevention funded the development of a simplified evaluation model to evaluate community health programs. The six-step process is geared toward helping communities understand evaluation so that they can more actively participate in evaluation efforts of their programs (The Center for the Advancement of Community-Based Public Health, 2000). Steps include (1) engaging stakeholders, (2) describing the program, (3) focusing the evaluation design, (4) gathering and analyzing evidence, (5) justifying conclusions, and (6) ensuring that lessons learned are shared and used. This is one of the key challenges of evaluation: engaging the community in the process by explaining the value of it, and helping them develop some ownership of the evaluation method and data generated from the effort.

Evaluating Collaborative Endeavors

The *process* of collaborative community research itself needs more intense study. A range of studies are needed to provide a more scientific description of the processes specific to communities and cultures (Koroloff et al., Chapter Three, this volume). For instance, the nature and definition of the intervention varies. What is the intervention really? Is it the outreach effort, or is it really the intervention itself? In one collaborative effort, an evaluation revealed that the control group also had positive results, perhaps because their only "treatment" was monthly phone calls, which the control group appreciated, so much so, that some cried when the project ended.

There are different degrees or levels of collaboration along 9 continuum. The degree of collaboration may be a function of the research question to be tested. At one end, the collaboration may be limited to getting a community to implement an intervention as is, without major adaptation or community input into the intervention itself. In this case, collaboration may be limited to networking and providing support and training to the community to implement the intervention. The purpose here is to test the transportability of a research-based treatment into a community.[11] At the other end of the continuum, collaboration relies heavily on community input into how to adapt and deploy an intervention in the community.[12] In this case, community involvement is critical to the development and adaptation of an intervention. The purpose here is to institute organizational change, a critical component of the collaboration because the ultimate goal is for the community to adopt and sustain the intervention. Each level of collaboration requires a different measure of progress. Some collaborative efforts lend themselves to evaluating progress by looking at the benchmarks that have been achieved; others may be more complex to evaluate because of the myriad of interventions and outcomes any one program can generate. The case studies below are illustrative of these issues.

CASE STUDY 19

Evaluating Collaborative Projects – Part I

J. David Hawkins and Richard Catalano

The University of Washington, Social Development Research Group

Mark Greenberg

Pennsylvania State University; Community Boards in 70 Pennsylvania Counties

One example of an evaluation of a large-scale community partnership is the Communities That Care (CTC) Program, implemented in 100 Pennsylvania counties. The CTC is an operating system communities can use to reduce adolescent problem behaviors. Under a five-phase systematic approach to community action and participation, communities begin the process by first assessing community issues, engaging key leaders, and developing a community board. The board creates an action plan and then selects, implements, and evaluates the chosen prevention programs from a menu of proven programs. By using the CTC operating system, communities can increase the likelihood that they will select and implement prevention programs that best fit their communities' needs.

A review of Pennsylvania's implementation of CTC focused on the process of evaluating the functioning of the community coalitions (Feinberg, Greenberg, & Osgood, 2004). The evaluation found that four factors were key to effective, well-functioning coalitions: *(1)* community organizational and motivational readiness to solve the problem at hand; *(2)* provision of initial training; *(3)* the quality of the internal functioning of the coalition; and *(4)* ongoing technical assistance. Results indicated that well-functioning coalitions are more likely to sustain their collaborative boards, and that well-functioning coalitions showed greater changes in the rate of youth delinquency in their communities.

For the past few years, researchers from Pennsylvania State University have been providing web-based evaluation for key leaders in each of the over 70 CTC communities in Pennsylvania. Each spring members of each community board complete a confidential web-based survey on how their collaborative is doing. These are then merged into a report for each local collaborative. Then, state-funded regional strategic consultants visit each site and present the report on current functioning to the local board on such topics as leadership, board communication, community relations, sustainability, etc. The board then engages in problem solving in how to improve their functioning. Thus, there is an action-focused feedback loop in which local communities both participate in the evaluation process and then use their reports for quality improvement.

Key Point

In this case, evaluation efforts focused on the evaluation of coalitions—how well the coalitions functioned. Well-functioning coalitions are more likely to sustain their collaborative boards, and importantly they showed greater changes in the rate of youth delinquency in their communities. Recent findings reinforce the effectiveness of this model (Hawkins et al., 2009).

CASE STUDY 20

Evaluating Collaborative Projects – Part 2

Helen Kivnick

The University of Minnesota, School of Social Work; The University of Minnesota College of Human Ecology; St. Paul's Hallie Q. Brown—Martin Luther King Center; St. Paul's Rondo Community Education Program

The CitySongs program is illustrative of the difficulty in conducting evaluations when the nature of the intervention, as well as the outcomes, might be many things to many different participants and funders.

CitySongs is an after-school music-and-development program for inner-city youth in the Twin Cities, Minnesota, founded in 1992 by Dr. Helen Kivnick and a diverse and committed group of neighbors and professionals throughout the metro area. CitySongs provides a high-quality arts participation experience for low-income children (without charge and without audition), encourages participants' families and friends to attend performances without financial barriers, and provides live performances to the community (http://www.citysongs.umn.edu). According to CitySongs, the goals of the program are to *(1)* grow *healthy, competent youth* in diverse and at-risk groups; *(2)* promote youths' *artistic achievement* and productivity; and *(3)* enable young people to help grow a healthy, vital, multicultural community and have a positive impact.

The comprehensive collaborative nature of the CitySongs program illustrates the difficulty in measuring outcomes, gathering data, and getting funds to sustain the program. Often, researchers may be hesitant to conduct collaborative interventions because they are "messy" and difficult to implement as well as evaluate. As in any intervention, relevant questions for evaluation focus on both the nature of the intervention (What really is the intervention? It is likely many different things to different people) and whether outcomes can be attributed to the program (And which outcomes should be measured: process outcomes or child outcomes?) The intensely collaborative nature of this program multiplies both the intervention goals and the outcomes under study, *some* of which are listed in the following text.
The CitySongs intervention is many different things, depending on each child:

- Public validation (singing in public can be validating)
- The shared experience of singing in a group
- Non-school teaching, learning, and honing of singing, music, and performance skills
- Adults who help you work to reach your potential

- Establishing a special relationship with at least one adults
- Exposure and briefings in connection with community-wide performance settings
- "Seizing teachable moments"
- Small-group and large-group time with social workers.
- Ongoing collaboration between adults across a child's life settings (e.g., CitySongs and parents; CitySongs and classroom teacher; CitySongs and pastor)

There are also many potential outcomes of CitySongs to evaluate, including the following:

- School attendance, effort, and achievement
- CitySongs effort and attendance
- CitySongs behavior (e.g., a member running out of the room to take a "time out" to blow off steam, rather than throwing a book or self at the wall, or finding some excuse to hit or otherwise distract some other participant, is considered a positive outcome related to self-control)
- CitySongs vocal performance improvement
- *Staff* descriptions and evaluations of individual youth behavior/performance/attitude
- *Youth* descriptions and evaluations of their own behavior/performance/attitude, of staff efforts, and of program experiences
- *Parent* descriptions and evaluations of youth behavior/performance/attitude, of program elements, and of staff
- Parental report of behavior at home
- Police record
- Longitudinal outcomes, including high school graduation, college attendance, regular employment, and stable adult family relationships
- The whole experience, taken together (e.g., retrospective, comment that "that experience, back then, really made a difference to who I am")

An annual evaluation is conducted that includes data from *(1)* externally conducted interviews with youth, parents, and volunteers; *(2)* written and verbal audience feedback; *(3)* CitySongs attendance; *(4)* school records; *(5)* interviews with children's teachers; *(6)* staff participant observation notes; and *(7)* social work/education participant files. These data are analyzed to provide information about program structure, process, and outcome with respect to each of CitySongs' three goal areas. Researchers gather data throughout the year, and this information is used to modify program delivery.

Key Point
Since CitySongs has three separate goal areas, different kinds of documentation support achievement in each area. CitySongs collects a wide range of data and provides it to funders as they require. New kinds of documentation data are added as necessitated funding agencies. Dr. Helen Kivnick explains,

Among the most difficult part of collaborative endeavors such as this are the time and effort it takes to maintain all of these relationships, and insuring the smooth flow of funding. While often it is nothing short of a Herculean effort, there are at least four big rewards: (1) strong collaborative relationships support constantly evolving program dimensions; (2) the need to maintain relationships with many funders and constantly cultivate new relationships means that the program's visibility and base of support remain broad; (3) there are great intrinsic rewards of working in a program that itself embodies a continually evolving community; (4) building and maintaining a community takes ongoing time and effort. This whole process continues to remind us of that fact, and to reward us with the experience of living in a community that is growing ever more tied together.

The Sustainability of Interventions

In many cases, the sustainability of a program rests on whether the program has been successful in the community. Community leaders will gauge the success of the program using data generated from evaluation. Once a program is deter-mined effective, sustaining the program becomes the challenge to many com-munities. Key factors to sustainability, illustrated in Case studies 21 and 22, include the following:

- The ongoing availability of *research data* that prove the program effective. Data drive the potential for getting funds to maintain the project.
- The creation of a *"home" or key driving force* behind the program. To survive, the partnership needs a driving force, such as a collaborative community board, to sustain the work.
- The *availability of training and technical assistance* for the community. Most community mental health agencies are underresourced, so bringing training and technical assistance to them is key for sustainability.

Extended Background

Funding, Data, and Evaluation

CitySongs receives no recurring financial support from the four collaborators' home organizations; they provide ongoing in-kind donations, moral support, and continuing community legitimacy. The annual budget is funded primarily through grants and gifts from foundations, corporations, government entities, and individuals (performance honoraria and T-shirt and CD sales constitute a smaller source of annual income).

CitySongs has received programmatic funding in domains such as youth development; prevention; education; after-school programming; arts and cul-ture; community development; diversity; underserved populations; and more. The year-end evaluation by the board and staff of strengths and weaknesses is used to make structural improvements in the program for the upcoming year.

Types of Data Collected by CitySongs

- Participation statistics
- Performance statistics
- Repertoire
- Special projects
- Social work and education activities
- Guest artists and speakers
- Volunteers
- Written audience evaluation forms
- Year-end individual evaluation interviews with kids and parents, conducted by external interviewers and recorded anonymously
- Indication of perceived excellence in the community (e.g., awards received, media coverage).
- Ongoing, timely participant-observation notes recorded by staff and volunteers and collected in a file for each youth

---

Most of the CitySongs grants are not explicitly tied to outcomes; because each funding source has its own programmatic and organizational criteria, staff document both that it has met (and will continue to meet) criteria for each funder, that it continues to make progress toward its own goals, and (for repeat funders) that is has fulfilled the previous year's program objectives.

CASE STUDY 21

Collaborative Boards and Sustainability

The Collaborative HIV Prevention and Adolescent Mental Health Project (CHAMP)

Mary McKay

Mount Sinai School of Medicine; The CHAMP Collaborative Board

While funding is obviously critical to community partnerships, collaborators also need to find a champion or home for their project, with thought given to sustainability from the outset. The Collaborative HIV Prevention and Adolescent Mental Health Project (CHAMP) is an excellent example of how sustainability was built into a collaborative program from the start. At the beginning of the CHAMP initiative, the CHAMP Collaborative Board, comprised of both academic personnel and community citizens and leaders, had the goal of transferring CHAMP to a community agency. In its mission statement (1996), the CHAMP Board indicated that:

> We want to increase communities' understanding of the strengths within their communities. If a community likes the program, the research staff will help the community find ways to continue the program on its own. (Baptiste et al., 2007)

In the CHAMP collaboration, this community agency was identified in the last year of the study: Habilitative Systems Incorporated (HSI), a mental health center located in the community. While there are many models for transferring prevention programs to community agencies, the researcher's followed these principles in transferring CHAMP to HSI (Baptiste et al., 2007):

1. Find a good academic–agency fit
2. Plan early on for sustainability
3. Continually focus on quality improvement
4. Identify the core elements that make the program work before transferring the program and balance the need to include these elements with the need to adapt them for a good fit within the community

As of Fall 2004, after 6 years of planning and preparation for transfer, CHAMP has been transferred to HSI, using the remaining federal NIMH grant funding. The first step toward transfer was the appointment of the HSI Chief Executive Director to the CHAMP Westside Board (the program will be replicated on the west side of Chicago). Four years of mentorship and training prepared leadership and staff for the transfer of the program. In the final year of the program, the program was revised to better fit the communities' needs and available resources.

While the responsibility for CHAMP has been transferred to HSI, more steps need to be taken to facilitate "full community leadership" of the CHAMP program, due to key challenges researchers encountered. During the transfer process, tensions arose from struggles:

1. To balance the demands of the collaborative process versus concrete project outcomes
2. To ensure that the scientific basis of CHAMP, including the research components of the program, are maintained, given that these tasks are a traditional part of HSI's everyday work
3. Between the differences in culture within the university setting, where HSI employees worked, were mentored and trained, and within the community agencies' culture and setting

Key Point

One lesson learned was the importance of identifying and involving the community agency at the outset of the collaboration, even before the grant application is written. In addition, a more thorough documentation of how the transfer of the program was done was needed so that richer, qualitative information would be available to review the process. Finally, an earlier determination of the necessary funding to maintain the program was needed, as well as better delineation of researcher's roles in the post-transfer stage (Baptiste et al., 2007). While many lessons were learned and much work remains to be done, researchers hope that the depth of the community's involvement in the project, as the shaper and messengers of the program, and ultimately the delivery vehicle through HSI, will sustain the CHAMP program in the years to come.

CASE STUDY 22

Training and Technical Assistance as Key to Sustainability

The Nurse–Family Partnership Program

David Olds

The Nurse–Family Partnership Program Peggy Hill, Nurse–Family Partnership National Science Office, Denver, Colorado

Patricia Moritz

National Center for Children, Families, and Communities, University of Colorado School of Nursing

The Nurse–Family Partnership program is an example of a comprehensive approach to helping high-risk families prevent negative consequences to infants. Over a period of 30 months, nurses visit homes and make an effort to help mothers and other family members improve their health behaviors, their care of the child, and encourage parents' personal development. They provide parents with child development information, parenting education, parental social support, parent leadership training, screening, and referrals to specialists. The goals of the program are to *(1)* reduce children's neurodevelopmental impairment (including emotional and behavioral dysregulation and cognitive impairment) through the improvement of prenatal health-related behaviors, *(2)* reduce the dysfunctional care of the child, which compromises health and development, and *(3)* increase the economic self-sufficiency of the parents by helping them plan future pregnancies, find work, and eventually, decrease reliance on welfare (NAMHC, 2001) The program has been replicated in three sites (New York, Tennessee, and Colorado) in diverse populations; results from the three randomized trials indicate that the program is effective, particularly for the neediest families (Olds, Hill, O'Brien, Racine, & Moritz, 2003).

Currently, the program is being disseminated across the country by The National Center for Children, Families, and Communities (NCCFC), a partner organization to PRC. The NCCFC provides community and organizational planning support and nurse training to help local communities implement the program. It also conducts evaluation/research to monitor program quality and determine what influences the quality and sustainability of the program in varied contexts. To date, over 150 program sites have been established in 23 states (http://www.uchsc.edu/sm/sm).

The program is especially noted for its efforts to provide extensive training and technical assistance provided by the NCCFC. According to researchers, staff at the NCCF focus on helping communities develop the capacity to implement and sustain the Nurse–Family Partnership Program (Olds et al., 2003) by assisting in the following:

> *Site development.* NCCFC staff teach communities the importance of having community buy-in and agreement on a problem, and the necessity of developing a plan to fund the program.
>
> *Staff training, supervision, and enhancements of the program guidelines.* Staff provide training to nurses in three segments over the first 18 months of the program. In addition, program guidelines are provided to guide the nurses' discussions with the families they serve. Sites are notified when guidelines will be adapted to reflect the latest scientific findings about predictors of maternal and child health outcomes.
>
> *Program evaluation and quality improvement.* Every site is trained to evaluate their program using software (the Clinical Information System) developed specifically for the program. Using this data, local sites can monitor their progress; in addition, NCCFC staff produces routine reports on the quality of the programs nationwide.

Several critical components of the successful implementation of the NFP include the following:[13]

- Nurse experience and maturity
- Nurse personality and attitudes; for example, it is important to be nonjudgmental and to have a sense of humor
- Some mental health training has been very helpful (also relied on supervisor and nurse prior training and experience)
- Having home visit guidelines as a manual to turn to for ideas
- Weekly supervision (individual and group)
- Time to share successes and challenges (one site had "retreat days")
- Model that allows for ongoing, lengthy relationships with mothers (as opposed to other home nursing jobs with limited time contact and brief relationship)
- Staff ownership of the program

Challenges in the implementation of the NFP include the following:[13]

- Organizing paperwork, data entry, and surveys
- Developing our own tools and brochures
- Sticking to the guidelines
- Client engagement in the program—retaining hard-to-reach families in the program

- Handling the discomfort nurses feel with sharing outcomes of implementation monitoring
- Making assessment tools more clinically useful
- Fiscal and political barriers

Key Point

This extensive training and technical assistance program provided to communities contributes to the overall effectiveness of the program. The program has been identified as a model program by the Substance Abuse and Mental Health Services Administration of the U.S. Department of Health and Human Services and the Office of Juvenile Justice and Delinquency Prevention, the Department of Justice.

CASE STUDY 23

A Community-Based Parent Advocate Training Program

Kimberly Eaton Hoagwood, Serene Olin, Geraldine Burton, James Rodriguez, Marlene Penn, Priscilla Shorter, Peter Jensen

New York State Office of Mental Health (NYSOMH); Columbia University; The Mental Health Association of New York City (MHA); and The REACH Institute

Many parents have difficulty in navigating the complex mental health system for their children. Consequently, parents may often feel frustrated in accessing adequate care to meet their child's mental health needs. To address these issues, researchers teamed up with the Mental Health Association (MHA) of New York City, a large advocacy and direct service organization for individuals with mental illness, and the State Office of Mental Health in New York State, to develop a collaborative intervention program to support family advocates in assisting families in accessing needed mental health services.

> To test the effectiveness of the training program and manual, 30 parent advocates were recruited from family support and parent advocacy programs in New York City and randomly assigned to receive the parent empowerment program or training as usual.

The Parent Empowerment Program (PEP) is a training program for "family advocates" aimed at enhancing knowledge and skills for effectively working with parents. This includes skill development to assist family advocates in training and educating families seeking mental health services for their children. Family advocates are usually parents of children with mental illness, whose role within the mental health system is to help other parents gain access to effective services and develop effective, collaborative relationships with mental health providers. In collaboration with community and state partners, PEP has been evaluated in community and school settings. The community is involved in *many steps* of the research process, including study design and development, implementation, and data analysis. The study is also structured to *support collaborative processes*; there are two project co-directors, one an experienced family advocate, and the other a mental health professional.

Initial findings learned from the PEP project (Hoagwood, 2006) indicate that parent empowerment training can produce changes in knowledge, skills & self-efficacy in the short run, but ongoing support and training are crucial for long-term effectiveness.

Key Point

Several challenges have emerged in the development of this partnership and program. The first is that a *substantial amount of time* is required to establish a genuine partnership. For example, the PEP manual was developed with significant input and support from researchers, community members, and policy makers. Manual development began as a result of discussions between researchers at Columbia University and the MHA in the fall of 2000. Immediately, parent advocates from the community were directly involved in the development and design of the manual content. Additional collaborators from parent advocacy programs and mental health provider agencies across the country were invited to participate in the development of the manual and significant feedback, resources and materials were contributed from researchers in the field. After approximately 2 years of development, all collaborators met to review and finalize the packet of four manuals; pilot testing of the manual began after approximately 4 years of development. The close collaboration between researchers and the community in developing the PEP manual and training program has resulted in greater sensitivity and a better match with community needs.

Another key point was the importance of insuring an *equitable distribution of power* in the partnership, including fair involvement in decision making, and opportunities to change aspects of the research process. The project was carefully structured to support collaborative processes, with two co-project directors— representing advocacy and mental health. The empowerment team, which meets bi-weekly, consists of senior family advocates, services researchers, mental health clinicians, and policy makers. No decisions are made without the input and consensus of the team. "Collaborative community research requires a combination of careful planning and humility," said Kimberly *Eaton* Hoagwood. "Most importantly, it requires the sharing of power in decision making and the establishment of careful channels of communication and structures for both listening to *and* incorporating feedback into your program."

CASE STUDY 24

Links to Learning (L2L)

Marc S. Atkins, and Stacy L. Frazier, PhD

The University of Illinois at Chicago; The Community Mental Health Council; Habilitative Systems Incorporated; Community Counseling Centers of Chicago (C4); The Chicago Public Schools

The mental health care needs of many children and adolescents remain unmet—as many as 4 in 5 American children do not receive the care or services they need. For those in high-poverty communities, the needs are especially great: nearly 80% of low-income children in need of services do not receive them, and of those who do initially seek services, many drop out of care (Kataoka et al., 2002). Marc Atkins, Stacy Frazier, and their colleagues at the University of Illinois at Chicago, in collaboration with the Chicago Public School system, have been developing and refining a model called Links to Learning, for delivering school mental health services to urban, low-income children with disruptive behavior disorders, a highly vulnerable and underserved population.

The overall goal of the intervention is to support teachers' use of strategies (effective instruction, classroom management, parent outreach) and parents' use of strategies (home-based activities, home–school communication) that are predictive of children's learning. Intervention occurs within a Medicaid fee-for-service system in which community mental health providers carry a caseload of children diagnosed with a disruptive behavior disorder. Also important to the model is the strategic use of key opinion leader teachers (Atkins et al., 2008) and parent advocates (Atkins et al., 2006; Frazier, Adil, Atkins, Gathright, & Jackson, 2007) to influence teachers and parents, respectively. This model derives from a considerable literature indicating the importance of children's schooling to their mental health and development, which is especially critical for children living in urban low-income communities where mental health services are scarce and schooling highly compromised (Cappella et al., 2008). Critical to the successful implementation of the model is the development of collaborative partnerships between the *classroom teacher, community parent, and mental health service provider.*

Links to Learning is built upon findings from two prior studies examining earlier iterations of this school mental health service model. One study called

Positive Attitudes toward Learning in School (PALS; Atkins et al., 2006; Frazier et al., 2007) revealed the critical role played by parent advocates who have helped to provide access to families in the community who traditionally do not engage in school activities or mental health services; enhanced the credibility of services in a community historically distrustful of university-based researchers and mental health providers; and assumed leadership roles in the development of and implementation of services to enhance parent support and education. The second study called Teacher Key Opinion Leaders (KOL; Atkins et al., 2008) examined the diffusion of information on best mental health practices within schools. Results indicated that peer-nominated KOL teachers can influence their colleagues on the use of recommended strategies. Parent advocates and KOL teachers both play critical roles in the Links to Learning model.

Key Point

Two key challenges have emerged during the implementation and study of Links to Learning and the school–agency collaborative partnership. The first is *aligning service goals with the missions of community mental health agencies and schools.* For a community agency, this involves conceptualizing children's schooling as an important clinical goal and determining that community outreach, in the form of school-based services, is consistent with their service delivery models. For school staff, it is often necessary to define mental health goals in the language of schooling and to confirm the importance of school success to children's long-term adjustment and mental health. The second key challenge is the need to *continually renegotiate the roles of all of the partners.* The roles of the mental health providers, parent advocates, key opinion leader teachers, and even the university staff, and their perceptions of their roles, have shifted and changed throughout the process. Teachers and mental health providers receive concurrent training on best practices for enhancing learning in classrooms and homes. The overall goal of the training is to cultivate a working alliance among the intervention team members, each of whom has a somewhat different role from the other, and to capitalize on the unique strengths of mental health providers and teachers by providing training targeted to new skills that will further enhance their role within the intervention team.

"The collaborative nature of the school–agency partnership clearly revealed what community parents, teachers, and mental health providers needed to help children learn. Links to Learning has taught us many lessons, including the importance of incorporating community context and sustainability into the design of a program," said Marc Atkins, L2L principal investigator. "A program has to be accessible, effective, sustainable (paid for), and supported by the schools and the community."

Notes

1. Interview with Dr. John Fantuzzo, conducted by Drs. Serene Olin, Ed Trickett, and Kimberly Eaton Hoagwood, 2001.
2. Interview with Dr. David Altman, conducted by Drs. Serene Olin, Ed Trickett, and Kimberly Eaton Hoagwood, 2001.
3. Interview with Peggy Hill and Patricia Moritz, conducted by Drs. Serene Olin, Ed Trickett, and Kimberly Eaton Hoagwood, 2001.
4. Interview with Peggy Hill and Patricia Moritz, conducted by Drs. Serene Olin, Ed Trickett, and Kimberly Eaton Hoagwood, 2001.
5. Interview with John Reid, conducted by Drs. Serene Olin, Ed Trickett, and Kimberly Eaton Hoagwood, 2001.
6. Interview with David Altman, conducted by Drs. Serene Olin, Ed Trickett, and Kimberly Eaton Hoagwood, 2001.
7. Interview with Nabila El-Bassel, conducted by Drs. Serene Olin, Ed Trickett, and Kimberly Eaton Hoagwood, 2001.
8. Partially excerpted from interview with Dr Leslie Whitbeck, conducted by Drs. Serene Olin, Ed Trickett, and Kimberly Eaton Hoagwood, 2001.
9. Interview with Dr. J. David Hawkins, conducted by Drs. Serene Olin, Ed Trickett, and Kimberly Eaton Hoagwood, 2001.
10. Interview with Dr. Mary Jane Rotheram, conducted by Drs. Serene Olin, Ed Trickett, and Kimberly Eaton Hoagwood, 2001.
11. Interview with Dr. John Weisz, conducted by Drs. Serene Olin, Ed Trickett, and Kimberly Eaton Hoagwood, 2001.
12. Interview with Dr. J. David Hawkins, conducted by Drs. Serene Olin, Ed Trickett, and Kimberly Eaton Hoagwood, 2001.
13. Personal communications with Drs. David Olds and Peggy Hill.

References

American Academy of Pediatrics. (2004). Retrieved on July 10, 2004, from http://www.aap.org/pros/abtpros.htm.

Atkins, M., Frazier, S., Birman, D., Adil, J. A., Jackson, M., Graczyk, P., Talbott, E., Farmer, D., Bell, C., & McKay, M. (2006). School-based mental health services for children living in high poverty urban communities. *Administration and Policy in Mental Health and Mental Health Services Research, 33,* 146–159.

Atkins, M., Frazier, S., Leathers, S., Graczyk, P., Talbott, E., Jakobsons, L., Adil, J., Marienez-Lora, A., Demirtas, H., Gibbons, R., & Bell, C. (2008). Teacher key opinion leaders and mental health consultation in low-income urban schools. *Journal of Consulting and Clinical Psychology, 75*(5), 905–908.

Altman, D. (1986). A framework for evaluating community-based heart disease prevention programs. *Social Science & Medicine, 22*(4), 479–487.

August, G. J., Winters, K. W., Realmuto, G. M., Tarter, R., Perry, C., & Hektner, J. M. (2004). Moving evidence-based drug abuse prevention program from research to practice: Bridging the efficacy-effectiveness interface. *Substance Use and Misuse, 39*(10-12), 2017–2053.

Baptiste, D., Blachman, D., Cappella, E., Coleman, I., Leachman, B., McKinney, L., Paikoff, R., Wright, L., Dew, D., Madison, S., McKay, M., Institute for Juvenile Research, & The CHAMP Collaborative Board. (2007). Transferring a university-led HIV/AIDS prevention initiative to a community. *Social Work in Mental Health, 5*(3), 269–293.

Bess, G., Allen, J., & Deters, P. (2004). The evaluation life cycle: A retrospective assessment of stages and phases of the Circles of Care initiative. *American Indian and Alaska Native Mental Health Research, 11*(2), 30–41.

Burns, B.J., Costello, E.J., Angold, A., Tweed, D., Stangle, D. & Farmer, E.H.Z. (1995). Children's mental health service use across service sectors. *Health Affairs*, 124, 147–159.

Cappella, E., Frazier, S., Atkins, M., Schoenwald, S., & Glisson, C. (2008). Enhancing schools' capacity to support children in poverty: An ecological model of school-based mental health services. *Administration and Policy in Mental Health and Mental Health Services Research, 35*(5), 395–409.

Center for Advancement of Community-Based Public Health. (2000). www.cdc.gov/Healthyyouth/evaluation/pdf/sp_kit/spt_pt6.pdf

Council of Program Directors in Community Research and Action website. (2001). Retrieved on August 9, 2004, from http://www.msu.edu/user/lounsbu1/cpdcra.html.

Eisenstadt, T. H., Eyberg, S., McNeil, C., Newcomb, K., & Funderburk, B. (1993). Parent–child interaction therapy with behavior problem children: Relative effectiveness of two stages and overall treatment outcome. *Journal of Clinical Child Psychology, 22*, 42–51.

Essock, S., Hargreaves, W., Covell, N., and Goethe, J. (1996). Antipsychotics in research and clinical settings. Clozapine's effectiveness for patients in state hospitals: Results from a randomized trial. *Psychopharmacology Bulletin, 32*(4), 683–697.

Eyberg, S., Boggs, S., & Algina, J. (1995). Parent–child interaction therapy: A psychosocial model for the treatment of young children with conduct problem behavior and their families. *Psychopharmacology Bulletin, 31*, 83–91.

Fantuzzo, J., McWayne, C., & Bulotsky, R. (2003). Forging strategic partnerships to advance mental health science and practice for vulnerable children. *School Psychology Review. 32*(1), 17–37.

Fantuzzo, J., McWayne, C., and Childs, S. (2006). Scientist–community collaborations: A dynamic tension between rights and responsibilities. In *Handbook of ethical research with ethnoculural populations and communities*, edited by J. Trimble & C. Fisher (pp. 27–49). Thousand Oaks, CA: Sage.

Fantuzzo, J., Stevenson, H., Abdul Kabir, S., & Perry, M. (in press). An investigation of a community-based intervention for socially isolated parents with a history of child maltreatment. *Journal of Family Violence.*

Fantuzzo, J., Manz, P., Atkins, M., & Meyers, R. (in press). Peer-mediated treatment of socially withdrawn maltreated preschool children: Cultivating natural community resources. *Journal of Clinical Child and Adolescent Psychology.*

Feinberg, M. E., Greenberg, M. T., & Osgood, W. O. (2004). Readiness, functioning, and perceived effectiveness in community prevention coalitions: A study of communities that care. *American Journal of Community Psychology*, 33, 163–177.

Frazier, S. L., Adil, J. A., Atkins, M. S., Gathright, T., & Jackson, M. (2007). Can't have one without the other: Mental health providers and community parents reducing barriers to services for families in urban poverty. *Journal of Community Psychology*, 35(4), 435–446.

Gardner, W., Kelleher, K.J., Wasserman, R., Childs, G., Nutting, P., Lillienfeld, H., & Pajer, K. (2000). Primary care treatment of pediatric psychosocial problems: A study from pediatric research in office settings and ambulatory sentinel practice network. *Pediatrics*, 106, e44.

Hawkins, J. D., Oesterle, S., Brown, E. C., Arthur, M. W., Abbott, R. D., Fagan, A. A., Catalano, R. F. (2009). Results of a type 2 translational research trial to prevent adolescent drug use and delinquency. *A Test of Communities that Care Arch Pediatr Adolesc Med.*, 163(9), 789–798.

Henggeler, S. W., Schoenwald, S. K., Borduin, C. M., Rowland, M. D., & Cunningham, P. B. (2009). *Multisystemic therapy for antisocial behavior in children and adolescents* (2nd edition). New York: Guilford Press.

Henggeler, S. W., Schoenwald, S. K., Liao, J. G., Letourneau, E. J., & Edwards, D. L. (2002) Transporting efficacious treatments to field settings: The link between supervisory practices and therapist fidelity in MST programs. *Journal of Clinical Child Psychology*, 31(2), 155–167.

Hoagwood, K. (2006). *Engaging and empowering families: Research findings on a service effectiveness study of a parent empowerment program*. Presentation at the 19th annual research conference: A system of care for children's mental health: Expanding the research base. February 22–24, 2006, Tampa, FL.

Hoagwood, K., Jensen, P., & Fisher, C. B. (1996) *Ethical issues in mental health research with children and adolescents*. Mahwah, NJ: Lawrence Erlbaum.

Hoagwood, K., Burns, B.J., Kiser, L., Ringeisen, H. & Schoenwald, S. (2001). Evidence-based practices in child and adolescent mental health services. *Psychiatric Services*, 52(9), 1079–1089.

Kataoka, S. H., Zhang, L., & Wells, K. B. (2002). Unmet need for mental health care among U.S. children: Variation by ethnicity and insurance status. *American Journal of Psychiatry*, 159, 1548–1555.

Leve, L., & Chamberlain, P. (2005). Intervention outcomes for girls referred from juvenile justice: effects on delinquency. *Journal of Consulting and Clinical Psychology*, 73(6), 1181–1185.

Lykes, M. B. (2004). Terror, silencing and children: International, multidisciplinary collaboration with Guatamalan Maya communities. *Social Science & Medicine*, 38(4), 543–552.

Madison-Boyd, S. M., Baptiste, D., Paikoff, R., Coleman, I., Bell, C., & McKay, M. (in press). Sustaining HIV prevention in communities: Researchers' perspectives on technology transfer processes. *AIDS Education and Prevention*.

Madison, S. M., McKay. M. M, Paikoff, R., & Bell, C. C. (2000). Basic research and community collaboration: Necessary ingredients for the development of a family-based HIV prevention program. *AIDS Education and Prevention*, 12(4), 281–298.

McCabe, K., Yeh, M., Garland, A., Lau, A., & Chavez, G. (2005). The GANA program: A tailoring approach to adapting parent–child interaction therapy for Mexican Americans. *Education and Treatment of Children, 2,* 111–129.

McKay, M. M., Chasse, K. T., Paikoff, R., McKinney, L. D., Baptiste, D. Coleman, D., Madison, S., & Bell, C. C. (2004). Family-level impact of the CHAMP Family Program: A community collaborative effort to support urban families and reduce youth HIV risk exposure. *Family Process,* 43 (1), 79–93.

McKay M.M., Hibbert R., Lawrence R., Miranda A., Paikoff R., Bell C.C., Madison-Boyd S., Baptiste D., Coleman D., Pinto R.M., & Bannon W.M. (2007). Creating mechanisms for meaningful collaboration between members of urban communities and university-based HIV prevention researchers. In M.M McKay. & R.L. Paikoff (Eds). *Community Collaborative Partnerships: The Foundation for HIV Prevention Research Efforts.* Binghamton, NY, Haworth Press, pp. 147–168.

The National Advisory Mental Health Council Workgroup on Child and Adolescent Mental Health (NAMHC) Intervention Development and Deployment. (2001). *Blueprint for change: Research on child and adolescent mental health.* Washington, DC: NIH.

Novins, D., LeMaster, P., Thurman, P., & Plested, B. (2004). Describing community needs: examples from the circles of care initiative. *American Indian and Alaska Native Mental Health Research: The Journal of the National Center, 11*(2), 42–59.

Olds, D., Hill, P., O'Brien, R., Racine, D., & Moritz, P. (2003). Taking preventive intervention to scale: The nurse–family partnership. *Cognitive and Behavioral Practice, 10,* 278–290.

Olson, A.L., Dietrich, A.J., Prazar, G., Hurley, J., Tuddenham, A., Hedberg, V., & Naspinsky, D. (2005). *Two Approaches to maternal depression screening during well child visits. Journal of Developmental and Behavioral Pediatrics, 26*(3), 169–176.

Randall, J., Swenson, C. C., & Henggeler, S. W. (1999). Neighborhood solutions for neighborhood problems: An empirically-based violence prevention collaboration. *Health Education & Behavior, 26,* 806–820.

Schoenwald, S. K., Sheidow, A. J., & Letourneau, E. J. (2004). Toward effective quality assurance in evidence-based practice: Links between expert consultation, therapist fidelity, and child outcomes. *Journal of Clinical Child and Adolescent Psychology, 33*(1), 94–104.

Simmons, T., Novins, D., & Allen, J. (2004). Words have power: (Re)-defining serious emotional disturbance for American Indian and Alaska native children and their families. *American Indian & Alaska Native Mental Health Research: The Journal of the National Center, 11*(2), 59–64.

Stricker, G. (2000). The relationship between efficacy and effectiveness. *Prevention & Treatment, 3,* Article 10. Retrieved on September 8, 2009 from *http://journals.apa.org/pt/prevention/volume3/pre0030010c.html*

Sturm, R., Ringel, J., & Andreyeva, T. (2003). Geographic disparities in children's mental health care. *Pediatrics, 112*(4), e308–e308.

Swenson, C. C., Henggeler, S. W., Taylor, I. S., & Addison, O. (2005). *Multisystemic therapy and neighborhood partnerships: Reducing adolescent violence and substance abuse.* New York: Guilford Press.

U.S. Department of Health and Human Services. (2001). *Mental health: Culture, race and ethnicity— A supplement to mental health: A report of the Surgeon General.* Rockville, MD: U.S. Department of Health and Human Services, Public Health Service, Office of the Surgeon General.

Wasserman, R. C., Kelleher, K. J., Bocian, A., Baker, A., Childs, G. E., Indacochea, F., Stulp, C., & Gardner, W. P. (1999). Identification of attentional and hyperactivity problems in primary care: A report from pediatric research in office settings and the ambulatory sentinel practice network. *Pediatrics, 103*(3), 661–665.

Youngblood, J., & Spencer, M. B. (2002). Integrating normative identity processes and academic support requirements for special needs adolescents: The application of an identity-focused cultural ecological (ice) perspective. *Applied Developmental Science, 6*(2), 95–108.

Chapter Six

The Future of Community–Researcher Partnerships: Headed for Impasse or Improvement?

Peter S. Jensen and Kimberly Eaton Hoagwood

About 15 years ago at the National Institute of Mental Health (NIMH), we began a dialogue with the field that resulted in a series of workshops and conferences about the importance of community collaborations. Some of this dialogue emerged naturally and perhaps inevitably, because of the pressures felt by anyone working within the Public Health Service to simultaneously serve more than one master: researchers—all of whom felt their work was of great public-health significance and deserved to be funded—and elected representatives who asked for accountability of precious tax dollars expended on research, as well as family advocates asking whether our research programs were going to have any tangible benefits in their or their children's lives.

In retrospect, it is both interesting and instructive that the first years of this dialogue with the field focused on ethical issues, beginning with a conference followed by an edited casebook (Hoagwood, Jensen, & Fisher, 1996). The central thrust of this initial dialogue involved researchers sharing their perspectives about how research with children could best be accomplished, while still satisfying ethical imperatives and the federal regulatory demands. Though many excellent points were made in this casebook, in only one chapter was the community partner/research participant perspective represented, and the closing chapter noted in passing the importance of community participants and investigators working together.

Later, in the mid-1990s, when NIMH began to emphasize ethnic and gender diversity—the ethical mandate to understand all human health problems (not just those of middle class white males), it become increasingly clear that there was no way one could approach the study of delicate, highly stigmatized areas without the trust and collaboration of families and communities who would join as research participants.

From the perspective of the first author, several critical incidents were turning points in this evolution. The first one comprised the most important professional discovery I (PSJ) have made over the last two decades. It happened while I served at the NIMH. This important professional discovery has also been for me a deeply personal one, yet I share it because it might be illustrative of the journey of the discovery that many researchers have made, including many of those whose research is described in the casebook portion of this volume.

The other two experiences occurred thereafter, one at NIMH, and another in the subsequent decade during my tenure at Columbia University's Center for the Advancement of Children's Mental Health. Both of these latter experiences impressed on me how much work remains to be done, in terms of the need for change in our attitudes and beliefs as researchers. Together, the three incidents demonstrate opposing sides of the same coin.

WASHINGTON, DC, FALL 1992

In 1992 the federal government, particularly the Public Health Service, was embroiled in a controversy about its so-called violence initiative. While many colleagues and I were working on NIMH's Multimodal Treatment of ADHD study (MTA), this study got temporarily caught up in the crossfire of public concerns and suspicions. Some zealots construed the MTA study to be "the smoking gun" of a violence initiative plot to forcibly medicate inner-city children of color. Then Secretary Louis Sullivan, MD, of the Department of Health and Human Services convened a blue-ribbon committee to review the types of activities being conducted by the Public Health Service, including NIMH. As a part of the committee's review, I went with then NIMH Deputy Director Alan Leshner, PhD, to answer the committee's questions concerning the MTA study design. Although committee members gave a clean bill of health to the MTA, I will never forget the words of one of the members of the prestigious committee that included African American leaders from all across the United States. To paraphrase as I can best recall:

> Remember when researchers wanted to do sickle cell research on us in our communities? There were concerns about the use of such information in harmful ways—restrictive insurance provisions, job eligibility, etc. What we advised them then was that given its sensitivity, sickle cell research should only be done within partnerships—by researchers who have teamed with members of our community. When you attend a sickle cell research meeting today, presentations always include a scientific member and a community partner. So shouldn't sensitive research—such as research on violence in our communities, where results can be so easily misunderstood and used by members of the community—always include both a research partner and a community partner? This would ensure that the research is sensitive to the political context, that results are appropriately understood, and that the results actually benefit the community.

It should be noted that the "violence initiative" as it was then called, even though it was developed in response to a general sense of public urgency and need, was *not* developed in concert with the communities who were most affected by violence or who would be the "recipients" of any broad-scale violence prevention programs. As a result of this experience, I became increasingly committed to and impassioned about the central role of families in crafting research projects that will be relevant to their community's needs and values.

Historically, mental health and mental health research have been the province of "the professional." Yet there has been a growing consumer movement in all areas of medicine, beginning in the 1970s, and increasingly affecting children and families vis-à-vis mental health advocacy in the late 1980s and early 1990s. This is described by Koroloff and colleagues in chapter three. Some colleagues might wonder whether families ought to be shaping the dialogue in current mental health services and even research, or why it should not just be left to "the professionals." But I have concluded that mental health research within communities, like violence, is one of those "sensitive areas" where full partnerships and trusting relationships are needed, in order for our communities (and our families) to take full advantage of what researchers have to offer. But it is a two-way street, and it affords us as mental health professionals and researchers alike significant benefits, in terms of increasing the validity, generalizability, and subsequent uptake and dissemination of research findings.

WASHINGTON, DC, SPRING 1996

The second experience, also at NIMH, occurred during a large summit of 90 persons on child and adolescent psychopharmacology. At this meeting a large group of researchers were joined by staff from three National Institutes of Health, the Food and Drug Administration, and other Department of Health and Human Services agencies. To this group were added the voices of a dozen family advocates, as well as a handful of ethicists, legal experts, and representatives of the pharmaceutical industry. The purpose of the meeting was to forge consensus among these key stakeholders about child psychopharmacology research: what advances had the field made to date, what research was needed, and whether and how the various stakeholders might work together to craft this agenda. At one point during the meeting, one researcher asked about whether research had been done demonstrating differential treatment response to specific medications as a function of gender or ethnicity, to which another researcher commented, saying something like: "That's not real research, that's PC research" (i.e., *politically correct*). An icy silence fell over the room, and no one spoke. My hope for an agreed-upon agenda seemed lost. But as the meeting host, I simply asserted that we all had a responsibility to ensure that our research findings applied to *all* children, and that the ultimate validity and integrity of our research was at stake. While the first experience emblazoned into me the critical need for *full and equal partnerships* with parents and community members in community research, the second experience highlighted how quickly we "experts" fail at times to take the community's concerns seriously, and in so doing, we unwittingly threaten the validity of scientific inferences and undermine our own efforts to apply research findings to communities. But what changes if we begin from the premise that the applicability and acceptability of research findings is as important as the findings themselves? The balance of power shifts. The power differential between researcher and community partner—from a narrow "doctor (or researcher)-knows-best" perspective to an enriched and more ecologically valid dialogue with consumers—is readjusted and realigned.

NEW YORK CITY, SPRING 2006

The final experience came after I left NIMH to found the Center for the Advancement of Children's Mental Health at Columbia University. I was hosting a high-level advisory meeting of two senior scientists and the CEOs/executive directors of two of the major national family advocacy associations. When describing some of my research activities, I mentioned the crucial nature of research partnerships with families and communities, including partnerships with national advocacy associations who represented many parents, families, and communities. To this one of the senior scientists asked somewhat incredulously, "What do you mean by 'partnerships' with families and communities, and why is this even relevant for research?" to which the other scientist replied, "Yes, it's not as though we are equal!" Pretending not to notice the dismay in the faces of the two family advocacy leaders, I explained as best I could why partnerships were essential. But there was little doubt in my mind that my words had little impact on the scientists. This final experience left me with the realization how ingrained and automatic are the hierarchical relationships embedded within medical settings, and how difficult it can be for researchers schooled in these older models to allow themselves to be educated by the community when taking research out of university settings into the real world.

WHY PARTNERSHIPS AND COLLABORATIONS?

In the final pages of this volume, let us again review the purpose and premises of this book, namely why researcher–community partnerships are so important. We believe that our families and communities are our "customers." All too often in the history of medicine, our theoretical models, including our notions of cause and effect (e.g., parents as causes, children as effects) are oversimplifications, are never fully correct, and sometimes are just simply wrong. Community members who become research partners often have deep knowledge of traditions, values, and embedded cultural norms that can affect in powerful ways community behaviors.

Given a context of trust and joint problem solving, community members who become partners with researchers and who engage in candid dialogue can often identify these hidden factors, and this can lead to new insights otherwise unavailable to researchers.

Second, the current emphasis on translational research—applying university research methods to larger populations—can only be accomplished by collaborative research with community partners. This new generation of studies must in essence move university investigators and their topics of study out of prestigious ivory towers and into everyday earthen trenches. This research demands new types of expertise—not with other scientists per se, but with local experts from families, neighborhoods, schools, and communities. Only from these experts can we learn what is palatable, feasible, durable, affordable, and sustainable for children and adolescents at risk or in need of mental health services.

The terms "collaboration" and "partnership" highlight the substantial changes that must take place in the traditional *research subject–university investigator* relationship. Historically, traditional investigators pose research questions based on a body of theory and prior research that constitute logical next steps in an elegant chain of hypotheses, tests, proofs, and/or refutations. These steps often isolate questions and specific variables from their larger contexts, in order to limit the number of confounds and alternative explanations of findings. Once the question and the methods have been sufficiently refined and funding has been obtained, investigators look for "subjects" (more recently called "participants") who will participate in the study. The quid pro quo for the would-be "participants" is often some kind of service rendered (as in the case of clinical or prevention trials), modest financial remuneration for the personal effort and time lost from work, and/or the intangible satisfaction from altruistic participation in a scientific endeavor. However, if one involves nonresearchers only at this point (as participants), the approach is not likely to be able to answer questions about the sustainability of interventions within communities; it is unidirectional (vs. transactional), fails to reflect the realities of community and interpersonal dynamics, and is blind to issues of ecological validity.

Contrast such investigator-instigated, university-based research with studies based on the kinds of collaborations highlighted in this volume. The traditional *investigator vs. research subject* dichotomy, essentially an expert–lay distinction, is transformed as *both* partners offer unique contributions and complementary expertise to the joint enterprise—rigorous research methods and technical expertise from the investigator, and systems access and meaningful connections to real-world problems from the community partner(s). Furthermore, factors that constitute "confounds" in highly controlled university studies become rich sources of variation in the real-world settings and can be viewed as useful challenges or "tests" of the feasibility, durability, and generalizability of the intervention. In real-world settings, these so-called confounds and myriad alternative causes and explanations for a specific set of findings are usually the rule rather than exception—hence the importance of replication over time and across settings, rather than one or two definitive tests.

Another distinguishing characteristic of research based on community collaborations is that research questions, rather than *necessarily* arising as a logical next step based on a theoretical framework and a series of incremental empirical steps, may be more likely to emerge from the practical needs and questions of the persons, communities, and systems involved in the collaborative partnership. Moreover, the actual nature and extent of the collaborations between scientists and communities may enhance the validity of the knowledge obtained as well as its real-world usefulness (Trickett, Kelly, & Vincent, 1985).

PARTNERSHIPS WITH WHOM?

Broadly speaking, as this volume suggests, there are three major groups with whom collaborations may be forged to move translational research ahead: First, policy makers themselves constitute an important aspect of "community." Thus, one neglected but critical area for new partnerships takes advantage of the clear need and importance of conducting research that will actually be useful to and used by policy makers, with the clear intent that research results might give shape to empirically grounded policies concerning child and adolescent mental health. Partnerships in this area can examine the extent to which current policies (local, state, or federal) are supported by research evidence, or perhaps even run contrary to research evidence. As illustrated in the casebook (see Chapter Five), such partnerships often result in merging of research and services funding streams across agencies or public-private groups, or in developing innovative approaches to current programs.

The second major "community" where research partnerships are needed is with "consumers." Broadly considered, families (both adults and youth), neighborhood leaders, school staff, and other community leaders are included within this area. The set of questions that might be investigated collaboratively could include the variety of roles that families have as active participants, not just in *receiving* mental health services for their children but also in actively *shaping* and *evaluating* them. This area has yet to be adequately studied, in part because researchers (and clinicians) often design a research or clinical program simply based on professional or theoretical perspectives. Not surprisingly, however, families (just like researchers and clinicians) do not like simply being told what to do, but instead want to be actively involved in defining the services destined for themselves and their children. Moreover, families and communities frequently have much different research questions than researchers, whose focus is often on a narrowly defined research study destined for a professional journal outlet as the main source of dissemination. New types of research questions could be examined if families were part of the original design team.

Furthermore, it is likely that research findings would be more meaningful, valid, and disseminable when this kind of partnership is formed with families.

Lastly, the third group of consumers is made up of clinicians and practitioners. They are often experts in what can be done in real-world settings and usually have a grounded understanding of the practical constraints in the delivery of care. Without their investment in the study questions and procedures, particularly if the study concerns a new therapeutic procedure that is to be delivered by them or their colleagues, many elegant ideas and study designs fail. While some researchers might regard more active roles of these three "communities" in research relationships as troublesome and intrusive, we suggest that the ecological validity and acceptability of findings from studies undertaken with this paradigm will be a direct function of the extent to which community partners were active participants in all stages of research.

PRINCIPLES OF EFFECTIVE COMMUNITY RESEARCH COLLABORATIONS

Given the need for these new research collaborations, can we identify key elements of effective collaborations? Elsewhere (Hoagwood, Hibbs, Brent, & Jensen, 1995; Jensen, Hoagwood, & Fisher, 1996; Jensen, Hoagwood, & Trickett, 1999; Schorr, 1997; Trickett, 1997) these principles have been identified and elaborated more fully, but we review several of the most salient tenets below.

External Validity

Traditional university-based investigations have generally emphasized the importance of internal validity, with the tacit assumption that once internal valid results are generated, external validity can be developed simply by "tweaking" the rigorously developed, internally valid methodology. Real-world research approaches that start from the vantage point that treatments must be optimized to be sensible, feasible, palatable, and sustainable, are seen by many traditional investigators as "too messy," intrinsically unreliable, and/or otherwise not replicable. We suggest that this implicit assumption that has guided much of the field (as well as the accompanying overvaluing of internal validity at the expense of external validity) is conceptually limiting, and sets an upper bound on the empirical benefits that may be generated from such research programs. Effective community–research collaborations balance and equally emphasize internal and external validity. Often, the community partner can serve as a watchdog to ensure that the chosen study strategies are able to generate meaningful and potentially generalizable findings.

To grapple more effectively with the issues of internal versus external validity, we suggest that researchers need to begin with different end points in mind as they design future treatment studies. Investigators must begin with the goals of developing therapies and treatment trials that are sensible (e.g., face valid whenever possible), feasible, flexible, and palatable. Primacy should be placed on these first four parameters, and only then should additional methods be applied to ensure the internal validity of the trial.

Incorporating the Values and Needs of Community Collaborators within Research Activities

Given the central role of consumers and practitioners in effective community research collaborations, the research partnership is likely to be able to identify and employ procedures or interventions that are palatable and acceptable to them, and consonant with their values. A lack of appreciation of such issues may do violence to the actual nature of the relationship between community collaborators and study staff, and possibly interfere with the study's scientific objectives. While "palatability" of an intervention is not an absolute requirement in every instance (most medical procedures could hardly be viewed as palatable), the child, family's, and/or clinicians' perspectives, as well as acceptance of and participation in the intervention process is usually a core ingredient of successful outcomes. Such factors, often termed "nonspecific therapeutic factors" in the psychotherapy research literature, reflect a human need to shape one's own fate—whether a clinician, a parent, or a patient—and to only carefully yield to other person a degree of control over one's life under conditions of trust. Yet in essence, in many of our research models, we often unwittingly assume an active, authoritarian role, as we attempt to deliver some predetermined product or agent to the consumer who is expected to passively receive it. In treatment contexts, difficulties in this process are seen as *resistance* or *noncompliance* versus a failure on our parts to understand the perspective of the person with whom we are working.

Can such approaches be taught and more explicitly incorporated into children's mental health research? Clearly yes, given the partnership models and case studies presented in this volume. Over the past 50 years various authors in the fields of anthropology, sociology, and community psychology have alerted us to the importance of the research–intervention relationship as a factor in research (Trickett, 1984, 1996; Trickett & Birman, 1989). However, we are unaware of any systematic efforts or accumulated research knowledge that addresses how such collaborations are maintained. Much rests upon the values and orientation of the researcher/interventionist, and his/her degree of native skill in communicating principles of mutual respect.

Full Conceptualization and Assessment of Outcomes

A third element important to successful community research collaborations is an approach to assessment of outcomes that takes into account the community partners' perspectives on outcomes (e.g., "consumer" satisfaction, quality of life, family burden, etc.—*consumer outcomes*), the child's functioning in home, school, and community settings (*functional outcomes*), the child's interactions with the larger environment (*environmental outcomes*), and/or outcomes that assess broader linkages to policy-relevant domains, such as services utilization and economic factors associated with interventions (*systemic outcomes*). As we have argued elsewhere, a comprehensive model of outcomes, such as the SFCES model, can be a useful heuristic to guide child and adolescent research (Hoagwood, Jensen, Petti, & Burns, 1996); unfortunately, only a handful of studies have addressed this range of outcomes (Jensen, Hoagwood, & Petti, 1996). Adapting the SFCES language of our earlier model to our expanded view of three different types of communities, "consumer" perspectives might in fact refer not just to patients and families but also to policy makers or to clinicians, to the extent that they are also involved as research participants.

Flexibility to Fit Local Needs/Circumstances

Almost no areas of medicine use a one-size-fits-all approach in treating illness. Thus, medication dosages are often adjusted to body size, the pace and order of cancer chemotherapies are changed to address individual patients' type and severity of side effects, and even surgical procedures are modified to be better tolerated by frail or compromised patients. Likewise, if university-developed procedures are intended for deployment within effective community research collaborations, they must often be adapted to make them feasible in their new settings, while still adhering to key *principles* that make the procedure effective. But procedures and interventions often must be retrofit to the specific needs, local resources, and customs of that community. Thus, while the principles of the intervention and possibly some specific aspects of the intervention may remain relatively constant across communities, specific strategies to work around obstacles, or to put local resources to work on the intervention, may vary considerably from one setting to the next.

Modifications of Research Methods

As noted by McKay (Chapter Two) and illustrated in the casebook (Chapter Five), a truly collaborative investigator–community partnership can lead to necessary modifications or different research methods. For example, random assignment to a placebo condition may not be acceptable and a wait-list control condition may be used instead. Moreover, given the importance of understanding the impact of ecological factors in real-world settings, and the complexity of these multiple interacting but "uncontrolled" variables, analytic methods and research designs for these settings must explore new methods, in order to fully capture the developmental or contextual phenomena under study. Under some circumstances more ethnographic or qualitative methods may be necessary to enable the voices and perspectives of citizens to be fully heard in the research, and to capture phenomena that appear to be present but are hard to fully operationalize. Because our research methods shape the endpoints of knowledge, insofar as either the methods or the content are superficial, important social, interpersonal, and contextual processes may not be captured.

Embracing Long-Term Perspectives

Another principle of effective researcher–community partner collaborations is a long-term orientation. Researchers with a short-term goal to test a given question or intervention program, and who commit "research hit and runs" once their research resources have gone, are likely to leave in their wake communities and citizens with initially heightened expectations and rekindled hopes, followed by bitter disappointment and hardened commitments to refuse future opportunities for research partnership. Thus, effective collaborations, whether with the individual family participating in a prevention trial or with a local citizens' board guiding a community-wide intervention, must be couched in principles of an *ethical compact* (Jensen, Hoagwood, & Fisher, 1996) between community partners and the research investigator, as they jointly work to understand and/or intervene with the problems of children within that community. In those instances where collaborations are most successful, this ethically grounded relationship will frequently transcend the time and space boundaries of the more narrowly defined, specific research project (Schorr, 1997).

CONCLUSION

We suggest that researchers and community partners must work more closely together to bridge the gaps between traditional university-based investigations and the research needs in real-world settings. Such efforts will enable investigators not just to translate their findings into practice (a utilitarian goal based on the researcher's agenda) but also to better address the actual mental health needs and to develop the most effective interventions for children and families in real-world settings.

Of note, research is lacking in several critical areas, and we encourage investigators to directly tackle these challenges. Thus, there are few actual studies of the research relationships themselves and how they affect the nature of the scientific enterprise (Billington, Washington, & Trickett, 1981). Also, while we have addressed what we *believe* to be important principles of effective collaborations above, in fact we lack systematic or comparative studies of methods for collaborating with communities, nor do we know how to encourage adoption of evidence-based practices within communities, once efficacy-based research is completed. Given these gaps, it is not surprising that we have no clearly understood or widely accepted models or typologies of collaborations.

We suggest that the high levels of public concerns and the frequent mistrust of science and scientists, combined with the increasingly active and empowered voices of citizens' groups, will soon evict traditional academics within academic ivory towers into real-world settings—that is, the "proving grounds of experience" (Barlow, 1981; Hoshmand & Polkinghorne, 1992). Community partners, and the larger group of citizens from whom they are drawn (and who vote, and either support or do not support research funding) will undoubtedly have an increasingly active role in shaping future research studies. If we are to maximize the value, validity, and viability of research findings, then these changes must be understood, accepted, and embraced.

Acknowledgments.   Portions of this manuscript were adapted from Jensen, P. S., Hoagwood, K., & Trickett, E. (1999). Ivory towers or earthen trenches? Community collaborations to foster real world research. *Applied Developmental Science, 3,* 206–212. The authors wish to thank Any Jensen for her insights and strategic input into key aspects of this volume, including the selection of the final title.

References

Barlow, D. H. (1981). A role for clinicians in the research process. *Behavior Assessment, 3,* 227–233.

Billington, R., Washington, L., & Trickett, E. J. (1981). The research relationship in community research: An inside view from public school principals. *American Journal of Community Psychology, 9,* 461–479.

Hoagwood, K., Hibbs, E., Brent, D., & Jensen, P. (1995). Efficacy and effectiveness in studies in child and adolescent psychotherapy. *Journal of Consulting & Clinical Psychology, 63,* 683–687.

Hoagwood, K., Jensen, P. S., Petti, T., & Burns, B. (1996). Outcomes of care for children and adolescents: I. A conceptual model. *Journal of the American Academy of Child & Adolescent Psychiatry, 35,* 1055–1063.

Hoagwood, K., Jensen, P. S., & Fisher, C. (1996). *Ethical issues in mental health research with children and adolescents* (pp. 287–297). Mahwah, NJ: Lawrence Erlbaum.

Horkheimer, M., & Adorno, T. W. (1972). *The dialectic of enlightment* (trans. J. Cumming). New York: Continuum.

Hoshmand, L. T., & Polkinghorne, D. E. (1992). Redefining the science-practice relationship and professional training. *American Psychologist, 47,* 55–66.

Jensen, P. S., Hoagwood, K., & Petti, T. (1996). Outcomes of care for children and adolescents: II. Application of the SFCES model to current research. *Journal of the American Academy of Child & Adolescent Psychiatry, 35,* 1064–1077.

Jensen, P.S., Hoagwood, K., & Trickett, E. (1999). Ivory Towers or Earthen Trenches: Community collaborations to foster real world research. Applied Developmental Science, 3: 206–212.

Schorr, L. B. (1997). *Common purpose: Strengthening families and neighborhoods to rebuild America.* New York: Anchor Books, Doubleday.

Trickett, E. J. (1984). Toward a distinctive community psychology: An ecological metaphor for the conduct of community research and the nature of training. *American Journal of Community Psychology, 12,* 261–279.

Trickett, E. J. (1996). A future for community psychology: The contexts of diversity and the diversity of contexts. *American Journal of Community Psychology, 24,* 209–234.

Trickett, E. J. (1997). Developing an ecological mind-set on school-community collaboration. In J. L. Swartz & W. E. Martin (Eds.), *Applied ecological psychology for schools within communities* (pp. 139–168). Mahwah, NJ: Lawrence Erlbaum.

Trickett, E. J., & Birman, D. (1989). Taking ecology seriously: A community development approach to individually based preventive interventions in schools. In L. Bond & B. Compas (Eds.), *Primary prevention and promotion in the schools* (pp. 361–390). Beverly Hills, CA: Sage Publications.

Trickett, E. J., Kelly, J. G., & Vincent, T. A. (1985). The spirit of ecological inquiry in community research. In E. Suskind & D. Klein (Eds.), *Community research: Methods, paradigms, and applications* (pp. 5–38). New York: Praeger.

Index